Hampden Gurney Primary School,
Westminster, London.

61

BDP. *CONTINUOUS* COLLECTIVE

11

Author: Hugh Pearman
with contributions by
Owen Hatherley and Lee Mallett.

Editorial team:
Hugh Pearman
Tony McGuirk
Julianne McAtarsney
Sheri Besford
Richard Dragun
Sanna Fisher-Payne
Helen Moorhouse

Graphics team:
Richard Dragun
John Beswick

© 2011 BDP

Designed by BDP

Printed in England

ISBN 978-0-9563523-1-6

www.bdp.com

BDP was founded as a practice of people sharing the opportunity and responsibility for creating buildings and places for all the people who use them. This book, which marks 50 years in practice, is dedicated to all those who have shared and continue to share in this endeavour, the clients who commission us, the users we engage with and all those in BDP who contribute, whatever their role.

Designers within a Collective Ethos
Hugh Pearman

One of the paradoxes of BDP is that it espouses a collective identity, and a certain anonymity of authorship, whilst harbouring some very strong characters and producing some singular buildings and wide spanning projects. If you met - as I did in the early 1980s - the people who had established the practice in 1961, you might have concluded that this was a personality-led concern. But the point was that there were many of them, from various disciplines, arranged in a regionalist manner across the UK and overseas, and they adhered to a culture of collective responsibility and a then unfashionable notion of public service. They still do.

Where did this ethos of the 'continuous collective' handed down through successive generations originate? BDP's roots in the working-class, industrial north west of England. Its founder, George Grenfell Baines, was the son of a railway worker, who as a young man developed strong feelings about equality and social thinking. Come 1961 the north west created a major cultural shift in the British and international scene as the Merseybeat hit the soundwaves and new directions in literature, theatre and television formed the new 'counter culture' of a modern generation. In this context of the re-energised north (and with a track record of industrial commissions) the focus of the newly created BDP made sense. Part of the

spirit of the practice was to do with making things, emulating the Bauhaus. Even its office in Preston was in a former biscuit factory - a burolandschaft conversion with its own gallery and music recital hall but that ran alongside the headline difference of BDP: its practical application of the notion of equality between all the professions involved in the built environment. BDP's manifesto was about raising design standards, through creative thinking, teamworking and processes, not dogma or style.

It might have seemed a somewhat counter-intuitive move, because this was exactly the time when signature architecture was on the rise, following the period of what had been known as the International Style. While Mies van der Rohe in the United States adhered somewhat to that doctrine, others - such as Eero Saarinen in the United States, Le Corbusier in France, James Stirling, and Denys Lasdun in Britain - were striking out in very individual directions. That fervent supporter of the International Style, architectural historian Sir Nikolaus Pevsner, was soon to be shaking his head in concern and muttering, by the early 1960s, about the cult of personality. But Grenfell Baines chose to go in the opposite direction, depersonalising his firm while remaining paternalistically first among equals. A number of other architectural firms also went down the team route around this time. Grenfell

Baines, however, turned BDP into the next logical step. Partly as a result of its north western origins, the way the practice developed went against the usual trend. For some years the BDP London studio, in the precursor practice of Grenfell Baines and Hargreaves in 1959, was something of a branch office. The main engine-rooms remained in the north; Preston and Manchester. The sharply ambitious, if somewhat homespun Grenfell Baines never strayed too far from his home turf, but, in his talent-spotting way, gathered gifted people around him who would travel to the ends of the earth if necessary. All this reversed the conventional professional trajectory in the UK, which is for nationally and internationally successful firms of architects to start in London and radiate out, not start in the regions and then take over the capital. To this day the practice remains a non hierarchical collective of city studios albeit London has become the largest.

Another working-class architect from the region, Norman Foster, has been compared to Grenfell Baines in the way he fought his way into a very middle-class profession ('a career that has striking parallels with Foster's' according to Deyan Sudjic's 2010 biography of Foster). Foster, who himself worked in BDP for a time, remembers working for Grenfell Baines over a weekend in 1958, helping out on a competition entry for Toronto's City Hall. Oh, to have listened to their conversation! Had the project been won, that would have been an historic collaboration.

George Grenfell Baines, founder of BDP, was fondly known as GG to all in the firm.

The spirit of the practice emerging from these origins has clearly worked. In the business of design, you don't reach a 50th anniversary in good shape if you've got your starting position wrong. Moreover - after a bit of a wobble in the market-driven 1980s when there was a danger of BDP becoming a more conventional, less integrated, even publicly-listed company - it is significant that it was the younger partners, then rising through the firm, who reminded everyone of what it was all about. They reaffirmed their faith in the original ideology of common ownership of a joint endeavour. Thus today, BDP is still owned by the people who work there, though the collective is given the protective wrapping of being a limited liability partnership. The wisdom of remaining self-sufficient and privately-owned is now clear: nearly all other practices who succumbed to the lures of the stock market in the 1980s (and many since) have vanished, or changed hands repeatedly to the extent that they are the same in name only. Architecture and design is a lumpy business that does not fit easily with the financial consistency demanded by outside shareholders. Besides - who are the clients? Real people commissioning real buildings for a real purpose, or city analysts staring at their screens? BDP has always opted for the former, while maintaining strong financial reserves to smooth out the ups and downs of the economic cycle.

It is not alone in taking this mutualistic stance, of course, and later in their different ways practices such as Arup, Edward Cullinan Architects and now Rogers Stirk Harbour and Grimshaw all have some form of common-ownership structure. At the outset, several of the large public-sector architects' offices of the time, most notably that of the London County Council, were also famously socialist in outlook, though they still tended to be hierarchical. BDP, however, applied the collective structure to the commercial sector, and moreover did so from the very beginning. Grenfell Baines and Hargreaves was a very successful practice in its own terms: but their leader took

the view that the best time for radical reform was at a time of success, not in a time of need. Nor was this a succession strategy, as it so often is: by then Grenfell Baines was still only in his early 50s. In contrast, his older contemporary, the great engineer Ove Arup whose utterances on the role of the built environment designer sometimes sound similar, waited until 1977, and old age, to put his company into an employee-owned trust. Arup had only added the discipline of architecture to engineering in 1963, two years after BDP had blazed the interdisciplinary trail, working from the other direction. For Grenfell Baines in 1961, then, this was a mix of heart and head, his socialist, egalitarian desire to create a British homage to the Bauhaus, coinciding with sound business planning from a position of financial strength. Idealist he may have been, but also a pragmatist. That's the BDP outlook.

Of course, the most immediately notable thing about the young BDP to its clients was not its collective ownership, but that principal calling card of being inter-disciplinary. Offering what to some was the outrageous notion of providing all the necessary services for a project, right through to product design and landscape, BDP found itself apart. At the time, this was not mainstream, and therefore not at one with architecture's ruling body in the UK, the Royal Institute of British Architects. Until then, architects had tended to be architects, engineers engineers, and so on with all the other disciplines. When they got mixed up, did that create conflicts of interest? Well no - just a better service. So while the institute fretted about that, BDP just got on with it, paying its staff's membership subscriptions to whichever institute they had professional allegiance to. Generally, what BDP tried first, later became institutionally acceptable: the practice came to be a kind of professional testbed for new ways of working, which are nowadays, of course, utterly proven. The firm seems somewhat aloof from the more clubbish aspects of architecture. It has the scale to have its own culture: it certainly throws open the doors of its London studio to the lectures and symposia of others, now hosting events by the Architecture Foundation, RIBA, and Academy of Urbanism.

This outsider practice grew to be the largest firm of architects in the UK, a position it frequently reclaims more years than not, as various pretenders to that crown fall by the wayside. It is always sheepish about the size issue, because it knows size for its own sake means nothing: and besides being interdisciplinary, it also knows it is a relatively small outfit compared to some engineering giants. But here is the thing: unlike some short-lived architecture/engineering companies which expand rapidly by acquisition - normally by hoovering up other practices of wildly varying quality in the rush for sheer size so as to deliver steadily increasing year-end dividends for shareholders in the good times - BDP has tended to grow (and recede, when necessary) organically. It makes acquisitions only rarely and very selectively, a good example being the merger with Lowe & Rodin in 1970. These were the structural engineers for the Metropolitan Cathedral of Christ The King in Liverpool and Jack Rodin, the principal, went on to become the first chief executive of BDP in the early 1980s. Sharing has therefore been a cornerstone of the practice's ethos and it still shares its profits among its own staff, business development, and strategic reserves. It does not hive sections off, though it does shape and reshape its studio network. The wisdom of this might seem clear, given the financial turmoil of recent years, but people too easily forget the lessons of history. In BDP's case, it has the experience of the economic switchback ride of half a century, as Lee Mallett describes in his later essay. The model works.

It helped that, back at the outset, the work produced by the young BDP was of such demonstrably high quality. As Grenfell Baines pointed out, a wonderfully nurturing working environment was of no use without talent. By no means has everything been glorious, but the practice has been a leading award-winner throughout its existence, in recent years being shortlisted for the Stirling Prize twice, and in collaboration

for a third. Of course most big practices are known for big projects, but BDP has become known for spanning scale and sectors. Its two Stirling Prize nominations are as far apart as a single form urban primary school and the regeneration of a large piece of a city fabric. Given its prolific output over the period, it doesn't appear to have had any of its work demolished unlike many contemporaries. The consternation among conservationists at proposals to flatten its 1968 Preston Bus Station, for instance - along with repeated calls to have it listed - shows how highly the best buildings of that early period are now regarded, as we see from Owen Hatherley's essay in this book. It is characteristic of BDP that the lead architect on the Preston Bus Station, Keith Ingham, was a graphic and product designer as well as an architect, and saw design as a totality.

1960s graphics poster for the new Preston Bus Station.

But how best to characterise the work down the years? This has always been a practice that is about spanning the design of all building types: not just cultural buildings, not just educational, industrial, domestic, transport, sport, leisure, retail, health and so on. After all, in the built environment, icon buildings can look after themselves: what's needed more urgently is for the base standard to be raised. The 'good ordinary' is a noble aspiration in building, because that implies the greatest good for the greatest number. Surely, this is what the design of the total built environment should be about. They can be background or foreground buildings, but the point is that they are user-centred. It is also very much a BDP thing not to be precious about the type of commissions it takes on. This might seem obvious now, but there was a time when there was a huge gulf between icon designers and commercial

designers: the former disdained commercial buildings (especially speculative offices and shopping centres) while the latter never got a sniff of the cultural and social ones. If anyone can be said to have bridged that gap over the years, viewing all building types as being equally deserving and tackling them all with equal vigour, it is BDP.

It's not enough, however, just to do good work across the piece, and to have an enlightened practice structure offering group working across the disciplines. To make your mark, you have to be progressive, show development in your design capabilities. You have to be capable of leading, not just following. I'd argue - not least because I've seen it working in action - that BDP's deliberately loose structure has allowed an environment where ideas can take root. It has always been a home for designers doing something unusual somewhere. Richard

Above: St. Peter's Campus, University of Sunderland 1995.

Right: Hampden Gurney Primary School. The UK's first urban vertical school.

Saxon, a previous chairman of BDP referred to it as 'practice within-the-orbit', which he elucidates as individuals running their parts within the whole. This BDP tradition goes right back to the beginning and Grenfell Baines' belief that talent should be allowed to flourish.

In consequence you can find some pretty radical BDP buildings - built and unbuilt - alongside some exemplary exercises in conservation and reuse. The 1990s University of Sunderland Campus on the site of a disused shipyard on the banks of the river Wear, exemplified the human approach to design espoused by Grenfell Baines. Furthermore, the urban game changing project that emerged at the turn of the millennium was the design of Hampden Gurney School in London. This vertical urban primary school promulgates a radical solution for the users' needs in schools in city centres (and keeping them in city centres). In turn, these two projects both led by Tony McGuirk, the present BDP chairman, led to a rich strand of progressive and award winning educational buildings. The practice's attitudes and enterprise towards regeneration of historic urban fabric goes back a surprisingly long way. For example; way before the 'Minister for Riots' Michael Heseltine kickstarted the revival of Liverpool's peerless but derelict Albert Dock, BDP had drawn up a 1970s regeneration plan to convert it as the home of the then Liverpool Polytechnic. This was a seminal intervention in the face of the all-powerful developer and architect combo that planned to demolish the buildings, fill in the dock basins and stencil a prosaic high rise office stamp onto the city's unique waterfront. Although the polytechnic scheme never happened, BDP remained involved and eventually the buildings and water basins were saved.

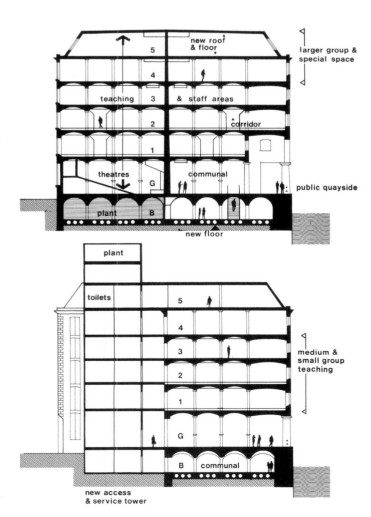

This page: Proposals for reuse of Jessie Hartley's Albert Dock for the new Liverpool Polytechnic 1974.

This led to a fertile strand of an imaginative conservation of mainly cultural and industrial buildings all over the UK. These projects show that conservation can be progressive, involving new people, technologies and uses.

BDP, like other firms, is not immune to architectural fashions - no design-based organisation with a steady throughput of new blood can be that. While some of its output might be said to be conventional enough, other parts of it can be almost defiantly radical. Rationalism and problem solving interwoven with humanist sensibilities. They have swung from Brutalism via Arts and Crafts revivalism and Scandinavian Modern to titanium-clad techno - with even a light touch of postmodernism at one point, along with most of their peers. Such things are what help root a building in its time. We must give succour to the architectural historians of the future. Grenfell Baines himself might have been described as a romantic functionalist, a description appropriate to other leaders in today's BDP. The only rule in the practice, style-wise, is: if you believe in it enough and do it well enough, then we'll see where it takes you. A system of internal crits ensures good ideas as well as overall good design manners prevail.

Top: Glasgow Science Centre. Titanium clad tecno shell forms regenerate the riverside with a new place for the city.

Bottom: Marlowe Academy, Ramsgate. Learning as theatre below the wooden gridshell canopy roof.

BDP has been known to collaborate in the past to realise major and interesting projects. It persevered throughout the 1980s and 1990s as Bill Jack, then chairman of the London office, and Jeremy Dixon, and later with Ed Jones and Nick Terry, worked together to realise London's Royal Opera House project. A variety of its professions with education experience jumped in to secure and realise Westminster Academy by architects (and BDP alumni) AHMM. This building went on to win the Sorrell Award in 2008. A year earlier BDP's architects headed a fully interdisciplinary team to win this prize, awarded to the architects for the Best Designed School of the Year, for its Marlowe Academy in Ramsgate.

A modus for collaborations, reaches an apt format for today the in the Liverpool One model, where the BDP masterplan was built out by a roster of good and very different architects, including six buildings by themselves. This creates the necessary variety and vitality of a complete city centre place. Now this anti-monoculture thinking is going further. Perhaps in future, should such a large project recur, the masterplan itself would be broken down and done by several hands. It's a discussion in the practice.

Arguably a personality-led firm would have problems here, the clash of egos being not wholly unknown in architecture and the other professions. Is it that BDP just thinks more long-term than some, knowing that, a few years down the line, the credit list is less important than the end result? Or is it just that famous pragmatism at work? As usual, it's both. Well used to being centre stage, BDP can sometimes be found working quietly in the background. I sense the ghost of Grenfell Baines in this flexibility. But remember - it's not just the lead disciplines involved here. Beneath the seeming canopy of architecture and engineering is inter-layered interiors, graphic and product design, lighting, acoustics, landscape, urban design, planning and sustainability. From the six partners present in 1961, the various disciplines would wax and wane, partly according to the prevailing client types. Public sector clients liked the all-disciplines, one-stop-shop approach; corporate clients were more inclined to pick and mix their consultants.

This is a firm which is better served by one of Charles Eames' bubble diagrams rather than a family tree. Design critics tend to find themselves liking this project whilst unsure about that one and not able to pigeonhole the practice - always an uncomfortable position for commentators. People in the world of architecture normally have firm views on what they think of well-known practices. Mention a name, and you usually get an immediate thumbs-up or thumbs-down. With BDP, it's more complicated. Is this variety, or inconsistency, or regionalism? It's clearly not design by committee, but neither is it wilful individualist architecture in the icon-building sense. The loose structure makes sense here. You are dealing with a self-contained design community which is a bit collegiate, a bit federal and above all, non-prescriptive.

Grenfell Baines was arguably the first modern British architect to integrate design and social idealism with the complexities of the modern commercial world. This is why, when he retired long ago in 1974 - with a flurry of significant projects on the books - BDP sailed on without a tremor, just as he had intended. Later on, when other generational shifts took place, it happened again. The structure of the organisation has always been about continuity - the continuous collective.

The emphasis on the design process, and the eschewing of a dictated style has created a fertile ground for BDP to flourish as a shipful of very different characters, all of whom - if they have the talent - are allowed creative freedom. But not so much as to forget the practicalities. As the elderly Grenfell Baines wrote in 1987:

'Handsome buildings that perform poorly are no more good to society than are good looking unreliable husbands or beautiful wayward wives to home and family. Ask the children.'

So those who look only for signature buildings miss the whole point of the BDP project. Too strong and ideas-driven to be anonymous, it is better regarded as a collective of equals, working in various fields towards a common goal. The BDP ethos is still idealistic, but here is the difference: if at first the desire was to change society, the model has also been very successful at adapting to society's changes. That adaptability - part of the long-termism inherent in the firm's outlook - has been crucial. Where, after all, is the building industry going today? Who controls what gets built? Why is the power of the architect steadily being eroded by other professionals and specialists? What can you offer in order to have greater purchase on the process, so increasing your chances of a successful outcome, for yourself and for society? One answer, and a good one, is to do what BDP first offered in a small way in 1961: provide a package of all the disciplines, a breeding-ground for individuals with ideas and a common purpose. As time goes by, it looks like a better and better idea.

Flexing with Time - Economic ups and downs
Lee Mallett

George Grenfell Baines' idea for a design business that deployed all of the skills necessary to build was a new business idea for the 'white-hot' economic and technological era that opened up in the 1960s.

Listening to GG's (as he was always known) soft-spoken irritation with his professional body, the Royal Institute of British Architects, for failing to share his youthful 1960s vision in some footage from the 1980s, reminds one of explosion of anti-authoritarian youth culture and counter-cultural idealism which flowered in the 1960s. Even though that idealism burnt out pretty quickly, and the 'white heat' of the early 1960s cooled rapidly, the same fate didn't stunt BDP's growth and GG's 20:20 hindsight was entirely justified. The practice prospered consistently despite Britain's economy spluttering like a dysfunctional firework for the next 20-odd years. We suffered enervating bouts of boom and bust and debilitating attacks of inflation - the highlight being the 1973 oil crisis. This hit Britain hard with black-outs, prolonged strikes, inflation and social unrest. From a promising start - and with a fabulous soundtrack - Britain declined to become 'the sick man of Europe' probably 'ungovernable' and 'drinking in the last chance saloon' - all popular soubriquets for Britain at the time.

Maverick, interdisciplinary BDP continued in spite of the post-war economic factors which conspired to undermine the structure of the British economy. The war had consumed Britain's capital, left its cities flattened and in desperate need of regeneration. Also during the 1950s much of our major industry had been nationalised while Keynes' dirigiste collectivist thinking ruled. We also had to pay back loan plus interest to the US, and float the pound as part of the deal. Our former colonial partners were now independent and had new business friends. These factors undermined the UK economy in the 1960s and throughout the 1970s. Yet we spent like drunken sailors, whilst failing to create enough new capital.

In 1961 Harold Macmillan told us 'most of our people have never had it so good', but this became increasingly hollow as the Tories and then Labour were forced to pursue stop-go economic policies to prevent inflation spiralling out of control. This had a curious double effect. Price increases led to intangible but demand-boosting perceptions about personal wealth. House prices began to climb more rapidly than they had ever done before. Laxer mortgage availability fuelled demand (BDP designed the Halifax's new headquarters in 1975) while the money in people's pockets and pay packets also increased. Society opened up. More women worked - and wanted education, while successful grammar schools were finding and launching a new generation of working and middle-class scholars who needed new university space. A wealthier population wanted many new buildings and the Keynesian economics of using public spending to float the economy sort of worked. BDP supplied the new need for new social infrastructure, helping to rebuild post-war Britain.

A new modernism in music swept from the north west to influence the whole country and the rest of the world.

Boom and Bust 1970. Rife property speculation runs in parallel with oil crisis and 4 day weeks.

The practice benefitted from the shared belief by both main political parties in free healthcare at the point of delivery and increased demand for better education facilities, and the political desire to provide them. This was the post-war political consensus between Labour and Conservative in action. BDP did well out of new universities and hospitals (Bradford, Surrey, and Ulster Universities, and hospitals in Nottingham and Boston). The need to repair town centres (Blackburn and Preston Bus Station) as well as create homes for new corporations (ICI, Halifax Building Society and Granada Studios). In fact, the whole of the UK construction industry was put on steroids in the 1960s and 1970s as we struggled to deliver new housing, new social infrastructure and a motorway and road system that could cater for a boom in car ownership and the birth of the consumer society. *The Property Boom,* by Sunday Times journalist Oliver Marriott and serialised in the paper described the vast fortunes made by the new breed of developer which caught the public's imagination.

The 1970s too were remarkably buoyant for BDP - the north had been resurgent for several years - the Beatles, the advent of Granada Television, the presence on our new colour TV screens of professional northerners Michael Parkinson and Bill Grundy. Series like Coronation Street and Z Cars all helped to establish a vibrant regional contemporary cultural and economic presence, which BDP was part of. The work, the Bank of England in Leeds, Halifax Building Society and the Northern Bank in Belfast gave the practice a new injection of confidence. All this activity was not at the expense of its beliefs in a humane architecture, however. The practice, for example, took great interest in saving the north's important heritage. Ken Moth, Jim Chapman and David Barnes, zealots in the Manchester office, worked energetically to reuse the great industrial buildings of Manchester and Liverpool.

BDP's general abstinence from speculative work for developers proved something of a prophylactic as it kept the practice out of the extremities of boom and

bust with which the development industry is periodically afflicted - the post 1973 oil-crisis being the most severe example before this decade's credit crunch. In the UK the 1974 crash was exacerbated by excessive bank lending to the property sector, which had resulted in the Bank of England's 'lifeboat' to save key banks from collapse. How endearingly modest that homespun analogy seems now.

The measure of how difficult to govern Britain had become by 1974 was that during Edward Heath's Conservative government of 1970-74, no less than nine million working days were lost in strike action. A brief period of calm arose after the election of Jim Callaghan and Labour in 1974. His 'social contract' broke down in 1978, leading to the Winter of Discontent which fuelled the election of Margaret Thatcher. Yet towards the end of the 1970s, as the consumer boom gathered pace in spite of economic ups and downs, BDP's size, national spread, expertise in town centre regeneration, reputation for good detailing, and more sensitive stance drew the practice into major retail schemes.

Above: Industrial heritage rediscovered and reused. Castlefields, Manchester 1984.

Rebuilding British institutions. Left to right: Northern Bank Belfast, Halifax Building Society, Bank of England Leeds.

URBAN RENEWAL – DURHAM

*Right: Durham
Millburngate unveils
a postage stamp to
celebrate important urban
renewal projects.*

*Below: Margaret Thatcher
becomes Prime Minister
in 1979 heralding a new
commercial era.*

Durham Millburngate was the first shopping centre to win an RIBA award, as well as be depicted with the Queen's head on a postage stamp of the realm. Work started on the sensitive regeneration and conservation of the Lanes in Carlisle. This more characteristic approach to creating new shopping and mixed uses, including a city library and housing, in open pedestrian streets and glazed over arcades was extended towards the mid-1980s with the Ealing Broadway project. At this point BDP was pre-eminent as a design firm in the revitalisation of town centres.

The advent of Thatcherism saw BDP become a much more commercial practice while the UK as a whole looked to the US rather than to Europe for inspiration. There was a wholly new approach to economic management - privatisation, deregulation, competition, acceptance of de-industrialisation, and the free movement of goods in Europe under the Single European Act and, of course in the City, Big Bang. The deregulation of the City made London the epicentre of international global banking. Thatcher's policies were fierce medicine though and the early 1980s were not pleasant - three million unemployed, riots and the miners' strike provided a dramatic backdrop while the economy turned itself around. BDP was sucked in to the capitalist dynamics of that era, coming close to being

a one-trick retail pony. There were no BDP education buildings and scarcely any hospitals, for example, during the whole of the 1980s.

Other substantial threads to the practice's work did begin to emerge though as the economy gathered pace. BDP's appointment to the Channel Tunnel project (many years after we joined the EEC in 1973) balanced its commercial interests and reflected Britain's new-found economic confidence in the future. Later there came the culturally prominent collaboration with Dixon Jones on the sensitive and controversial yet highly successful redevelopment and refurbishment of the Royal Opera House in Covent Garden. This was no mean feat in the anti-modernist, conservationist atmosphere of the 1980s and early 1990s. It took 17 years to complete and was partly funded by the Millennium Commission set up under Thatcher's successor, John Major, to spend National Lottery money on projects for the Millennium. Both the Channel Tunnel and the Royal Opera House were large-scale projects that Britain had been unable to contemplate in the threadbare 1960s and 1970s and were symbols of the UK's economic resurgence. BDP's Channel Tunnel project had in itself an office scale interdisciplinary team of 120 people on its own.

Above left: Continental Shift. UK Channel Tunnel Terminal Folkestone. Britain integrates into the European network 1994.

Above right: The Royal Opera House, Covent Garden London. The reuse of the Floral Hall for the 'people's performance'.

Cribbs Causeway, outside Bristol, completed in the 1990s was the last of the out-of-town shopping malls of this era. For BDP it marked the beginning of a more reflective phase and the Tories adjusted planning policy to shut the stable door. The recession of the early 1990s brought on by the excesses of the 1980s prompted further contemplation. The practice was caught out by the pitfalls it had managed to avoid in the 1960s and 1970s.

As with many other businesses, a bonfire of the vanities ensued. Staff more than halved from 1200 to 500 as the economy went into melt-down. Sectors within the practice were cut as equally as possible and this enabled a younger stratum of designers to rise to the fore. The practice returned to its roots and sought education work again to broaden its practice base and the new conversion of polytechnics into universities helped propel this. The first major project in this new dawn was for Sunderland University. Sunderland became an exemplar in its field with open accessible learning methods and the use of IT at the heart of new pedagogical methods. The highest ranked university, Cambridge University went to look at Sunderland, one of the lowest ranked, and subsequently commissioned from BDP a series of high-quality low-cost academic buildings. The emerging global economy, driven by IT, was affecting every aspect of life. This conjoined sectors and diversification became part of BDP's culture again.

*Left: Cribbs Causeway,
Bristol 1998. A finale for the
out of town big shopping
centres in the UK.*

*Below: University of
Cambridge, Faculty
of Education. British
sustainable design for
one of Britain's leading
academic institution 2003.*

Above: Rooftop
Technology Garden,
Hampden Gurney School
designed 1994 - 2002.
A forerunner to the
schools' renewal
programme in the UK.

Right: Tony Blair becomes
Prime Minister as leader of
New Labour 1997. 'Education,
Education, Education' the
immortal words to herald
in the schools' renewal
programme.

The arrival of New Labour in 1997 after 18 years of Tory rule opened up a new era of expansion for an improved BDP which had returned to its roots. Tony Blair and Gordon Brown welded Tory economic policy to a social agenda, maintaining fiscal continence - at least until the noughties. This encouraged further economic growth and enabled a programme of revitalisation of Britain's health and education services. A boom was born and BDP grew rapidly again. Schools, hospitals, cultural and sporting projects all followed alongside commercial and residential projects.

The project that best exemplified the new BDP which emerged from the 1990s into the noughties was Hampden Gurney School in Marylebone, London. It also exemplified so many things that were to become the hallmark of Britain under New Labour and the economic forces at work in the UK. It was a mixed education and residential scheme that replaced a 1950s school. It was inner city regeneration that not only renewed buildings, but transformed aspects of the local community - evidenced in its popularity and educational achievements. Hampden Gurney provided BDP with a great exemplar just as the Building Schools for the Future and Academies programmes of government spending took off.

Retail schemes made a comeback too, in Sheffield and at Liverpool One - the major retail regeneration scheme of the noughties. The practice also made a successful attempt to get back into healthcare just as the major PFI initiative took off.

There is a strong sense that as BDP contemplates the 21st century's global marketplace it does so from a similar point of view to the one it held in 1961 - a broad, populist, benign, pragmatic, thinking provider in a world that needs quality building design services. There are now over 1000 people in 16 studios around the world. Now set up in the Netherlands, Abu Dhabi, India and China, it looks towards North America with new projects in Toronto. Its European outlook and expertise in sustainable design and architecture being highly valued around the world.

Despite the global economic downturn, George Grenfell Baines' vision has created a platform for architectural business which fits the global marketplace. Perhaps most importantly, BDP has retained and developed its own distinct culture. It is a culture rooted in a social utility that has been rescued and refurbished at least once in the practice's history. This achievement, in purely business terms, allows BDP to occupy the position it does, and has created one of the world's most powerful architectural brands - which is probably not how GG would have described it. But in today's intensely capitalist marketplace, that social utility is the engine of what BDP has achieved and will achieve in the future.

Nanjing Medical University, China 2010.
Taking humane user centred design for
learning to dramatic effect.

The Collective Idea
Owen Hatherley

Collective Architecture for a Collective Society

After 1945, Britain threatened to become an egalitarian, modernist society. Ideas had been bubbling away about collectivity, art for the masses, and the possibility of replanning whole cities on modern and humanist principles through much of the 1930s. In film, for instance, there was the Post Office's GPO Film Unit, where animators and documentary makers were given free rein to create experimental work under the banner of public service; in architecture, there were collectives and organisations like MARS, a group of modernists in the decade of Tudorbethan who established links with their more successful continental compatriots, the Bauhaus and Le Corbusier; while a wave of emigration led to the brief residence in the UK of various Bauhaus teachers. This itself wasn't radical enough for some, like the Anglo-Soviet architect Berthold Lubetkin and his Tecton group, who set up an 'Architects and Technicians Organisation' to avoid any suspicion of narrow architectural bias. George Grenfell Baines formed his firm Grenfell Baines and Hargreaves at this time, and based it on strongly socialist collective principles. The Bauhaus model was his inspiration taking it further by adding in the technologies of engineering, environmental, civil and structural as well as town planning. This interdisciplinary collective idea formed the kernel of the practice that emerged as Building Design Partnership, better known nowadays as BDP.

It was amongst this 19th century urban landscape of terraced housing and mills that BDP opened its office.

After 1945 this new generation came to power, and not just in architecture. Under the social democratic consensus that lasted until 1979, there was what in retrospect seems like a movement towards popular education, towards collectivity, and towards an upsetting of hierarchies. This can be seen in everything from Penguin Books, with their educational but non-patronising subject matter and their crisp modernist design, to the new 'plate-glass universities' (and even more, the Open University), to the musique concrete for the masses composed by the BBC Radiophonic Workshop. Yet more than anything else, this movement could be seen in architecture, planning and design. Under the Labour government of Clement Attlee, these architects and planners were finally allowed to design whole new towns (BDP designing Newton Aycliffe), to rehouse the poor, and to try and design for a collective society. For some, this entailed a complete revision of

how architecture itself was practised, and it's the effort to change this undertaken by Building Design Partnership that will be the focus here - though as a part of a wider movement, rather than lone innovators, as is purported by many of the individualist architects of today.

Architecture is not, whatever the currently popular notion of 'starchitects' would imply, like the other arts. More than anything else, it is an art form dictated by capital and collaborative working. While we might cheerfully ascribe a building to Norman Foster or Le Corbusier, we know full well that it was the product of tens, maybe hundreds of different people. Sometimes, in cases where the originally named founders are long dead or have thoroughly put down their pencils, this is taken to almost comic extremes; take for instance the fact that we refer to the extraordinary series of ecclesiastical and educational buildings designed by Isi Metzstein and Andy MacMillan in the 1950s-1970s as being the work of Gillespie Kidd & Coia. Yet, the ambiguous popularisation and exclusivity of architecture in the late 1990s and 2000s, the post-industrial process kicked off by Gehry's Bilbao Guggenheim, meant that the famous architect was now treated as a combination of a CEO and a tortured artist. It's especially funny that this occurred at the point where the most famous artists were outsourcing the actual labour of their work to contractors. Yet, from the 1920s onwards, intensifying after 1945 and reaching a sort of culmination in the early BDP, was a movement in architecture and design to accentuate collectivity, to make a virtue of this architectural necessity. This was linked to a very particular politics - a notion of using progress for the collective good.

Penguin Books, looking forward with Mod-ernistic graphics.

Collaboratives, Co-Operatives, Co-Partnerships and Councils

'My home background and voracious reading gave a strong leftward inclination to my views of life. From these, sharing as an ideal, sharing not just what we have but, more importantly, each shares in contributing effort to making it. One great discovery was of Walter Gropius and his bringing together of artists, sculptors, industrial designers, photographers, and architects in an attempt to create a unity of arts and technology. Learning of this brought a flash of inspiration to my own experience. What had only been sensed darkly became brilliantly clear. Why not do this with the building industry and the professions? Group practices of all the disciplines! Technology and Art linking together in fruitful dialectic relationships!'

George Grenfell Baines

It starts at the Bauhaus, with the school set up in the chaotic aftermath of the German revolution of 1918, pledged to erect the 'Cathedral of Socialism', with architects, artists and designers of everything from fabrics to type helping to contribute to it. This was all the more true when the school moved from the elite outpost of Weimar to the industrial boomtown of Dessau; this grimy industrial town reminiscent of northern England was a context that would have inspired Grenfell Baines founding BDP, his collective design group in Preston - one of the first industrial towns. The Bauhaus' extraordinary headquarters was completed in 1926, yet unfortunately only partly fulfilled the promises of collective co-operation as part of a new society. For one thing, it was (and is) actually two separate buildings, with the Bauhaus clearly demarcated from the more lowly Dessau Polytechnic, and Walter Gropius himself very clearly identified as the designer. In fact, he had a large part of the famous skyway that linked the two buildings as his own independent architectural office, and when he left the school in 1928 it was in order to concentrate on that increasingly lucrative sideline. If there is a way the Bauhaus predicts the possibility of a truly interdisciplinary design, where the architect himself is almost of secondary importance, it's through the period where the school was run by the second and least famous of its directors, Hannes Meyer. The Swiss Meyer had been known for his work in the Co-Operative movement, where he had designed the co-operative Friedorf estate, in Basel. In a series of trenchant essays, such as *The New World,* he wrote of the obsolescence of old ideas about art and architecture in the era of mass production, cinema, radio, co-ops and trade unions.

The Bauhaus Headquarters, Dessau 1926. The Bauhaus aimed to fulfil the promise of collective co-operation as part of a new society.

Poster demonstrating early characteristics of the 'New Typography', designed by Joost Schmidt for the first Bauhaus exhibition in 1923.

Today, Meyer is remembered partly for his communist sympathies, for being sacked from the school for donating college monies to striking miners, and for his aggressive assertions that architecture, as a 'fine art', a discipline in its own right, produced by an identifiable individual, in a signature style, was utterly irrelevant to the preoccupations of the egalitarian industrial society he hoped Weimar Germany was becoming. Architecture, for Meyer and his supporters, was an anachronism, and until Philip Johnson and Henry-Russell Hitchcock tried to recuperate it as the International Style, 'an architecture still' for American consumption, this international modernism was known as the Neues Bauen, the New Building, or sometimes as Constructivism - but the 'A' word was avoided as much as possible. That concentration on 'building' over 'architecture' as the way of constructing a modern society was to have an inadvertent legacy in BDP decades later.

Two building complexes were credited specifically to the Bauhaus itself, although it was known that Hannes Meyer and Hans Wittwer were the head designers. They still stand today, in a sometimes slightly forlorn form. The ADGB-Schule in Bernau, on the north eastern outskirts of Berlin, was essentially a weekend school in the woods for Trade Unionists (ADGB was the German TUC). This unpretentious building is a series of boxes containing halls of residence and classrooms descending down a shallow slope, detailed in a rough, unshowy brick, linked by a far more extraordinary system of circulation via a covered walkway. Inside, specially designed lighting, doors and teaching equipment were operated at the touch of a button, with a subtle use of colour-coding intended to induce a 'psychotechnical' effect on the socialist autodidacts using the building. There was only one remotely 'iconic' moment that the anonymous Bauhaus collective allowed themselves - three factory chimneys announcing the presence of the industrial classes in this genteel rural outpost. These were lost in the 1950s, but the rest of the building was recently restored as an educational facility. The ADGB

School is an enduringly excellent building, but the other collective work is more ambiguous - an expansion of the Dessau-Torten council estate. This began in 1926 with an experimental first phase by Gropius, attempting the use of assembly line principles to build modernist family houses - cubic, flat-roofed terraces, aesthetically relieved by subtle use of colour and geometry. Meyer and the Bauhaus brigade were hired by the local council to extend the estate, and they junked first of all the concept of single-family houses, opting for something more communal - deck-access flats, with a glazed stairtower in the middle. The new extensions were a straightforward brick construction akin to work by the London County Council Architects' Department from the 1930s. Functionally decent, they lacked the pizzazz and striking strangeness of Gropius' work. The new Bauhaus Architects' Department was in principle anonymous, out of disdain for the famous architect. But did this mean the buildings it created would have to be anonymous too?

Meyer's claim that collective working need not result in monotony was, ironically, later vindicated by Gropius. After the war, Gropius dissolved his private practice, which for a period had become more important than the Bauhaus itself, into The Architects' Collaborative (TAC) - a co-operation of former students of his from Harvard. This rarefied terrain was a very different environment for such an experiment in collectivity, certainly more than left-leaning industrial towns like Dessau and Preston. But Gropius' riposte to any associated anonymity of collectiveness was exemplified in the likes of TAC's housing at Hansaviertel, West Berlin, sitting colourfully and vividly alongside work by Niemeyer and Aalto. A more notorious work undertaken by TAC was the PanAm building in New York. This was a building which, at the time, embodied for the baby-boomers the curdled promise of modernism. It was widely reviled as a corporate monolith blocking views and destroying public transport. With Gropius, then, the jury on the virtues of collectivity might be out, with the collective arguably becoming the corporate.

'When BDP was well established, I had the chance to visit Gropius at Harvard and tell him what we had achieved, "You have done what I would have liked to have done at Dessau" he said. Just then I felt I had turned to look down from the mountain, realising how far we had climbed'.

George Grenfell Baines

ADGB School, Bernau 1930.
One of the most eminent
Bauhaus buildings.

If anything, the Bauhaus ideas were being better implemented elsewhere - in the post-war UK, in the cities Gropius once dismissed as 'deserts of brick'. First and foremost, this was via the local authorities who had built thousands of traditionalist closes or stock-brick deck-access flats in the inter-war years. Post-war reconstruction coincided with the victory of the modernists who had lobbied throughout the 1930s - the architecture associated with what Orwell called 'the deep sleep of England' in that decade, Mock Tudor, Neo-Georgian and commercial art deco - was rejected along with its politics, with the Labour landslide of 1945, with a wave of nationalisations and the establishment of a Welfare State. Perhaps the first built example of this was in emergency architecture - the prefabs, temporary replacements for bombed out housing. These found a more permanent form in the Hertfordshire Schools, small, partly prefabricated modernist buildings in the capital's commuter belt, explicitly influenced both by Gropius' writings on prefabrication in *The New Architecture and the Bauhaus*, and the oddly contextual, restrained, brick style of his Impington Village College in Cambridgeshire.

The city councils at the forefront of the new architectural collectivity were London and, Sheffield, both avoided standardisation, instead tailoring their designs to specific sites. These managed to accommodate stylistic range and often infighting, most famously found in the Alton Estate in Roehampton, torn between the informal, Scandinavian east side, of coloured tiles, winding pathways and pitched roofs - derided by its opponents as 'people's detailing', in reference to the architects' communist sympathies; and Alton West, a 'hard-line Corbusian' area of geometrically arranged slab blocks and cubic, stepped old people's homes. Regardless of the aggressive originality of some of the buildings, and the clear stylistic demarcation, all of it was credited to the same faceless collective group - the London County Council Architects Department. For that, many of its architects - Leslie Martin, Robert Matthew, Colin St John Wilson, Ron Herron, Rodney Gordon - would become much more famous in their extracurricular work). In Sheffield, the case was even more marked, where a left-wing Labour council embarked simultaneously upon the picturesque planning of Gleadless Valley and the Brutalist monumentalism of Hyde Park and Park Hill.

In the aftermath of 1945, the context in which the founding ideas of BDP took root was one of complex and sometimes thwarted experiments in collectivity and co-operation. Interestingly several private architects tried to transfer the collective approach they had learned in the new social programmes into their work away from the council architects' departments. This could partly be seen in the new, depersonalised firms created by leading modernists. Yorke Rosenberg & Mardall was formed by Bauhaus teacher Marcel Breuer's former partner, FRS Yorke. RMJM was created by the LCC's Robert Matthew and Hertfordshire Council's Stirrat Johnson-Marshall. The firm which seemed to have taken Gropius most to heart was the Architects Co-Operative Partnership, formed in the 1940s by a group of former Architectural Association students in London. This practice as Alan Powers writes, 'aimed, through an anonymous group practice, to avoid the egotism of an earlier generation and, like architects in public service, to become part of a shared movement based on research and openness to experiment'. In their design of the Brynmawr Rubber Factory in South Wales, the organisation of the plant tried to break down the divide between management and workers. Later, dropping the more politicised part of their name, they became the Architects Co-Partnership, specialising in educational buildings. Their most notorious work was primarily famous for what went on inside the building rather than the outside - the Risinghill Comprehensive School in Islington, North London was noted for its experimental non-hierarchical teaching, with co-operation between teachers and pupils. It was closed by the London County Council in 1965 after a press campaign against it, although many of its ideas are now widely accepted.

Early collectives: London County Architects' Department. Roehampton's counterpoint design languages: Alton East - informal Scandinavian groups and 'people's detailing'. Alton West - Corbusian, hard line cubic slab blocks.

'What's an Architect?' George Grenfell Baines

There's an accepted story about post-war modernism, and why it apparently succeeded with the politicians and failed with the public, and it centres on the class divide between the architects and those they were professedly designing a new world for. Think of all those 1930s documentaries where stiff men in tweed suits declaim in RP on the unbearable conditions in the slums, on the need for hygiene, light, air and openness, or of the widespread canard that modernist architects always live in Georgian houses. Here, modernism is de haut en bas, a let-them-eat-cake solution to a housing crisis where former inner city dwellers are rehoused in obsessively sanitary but soulless new towns and high-rises, by people who would never have lived either in the old back-to-backs nor in the new towers - who preferred that others had to suffer the consequences of their experiments. What is so striking about George Grenfell Baines is that he fits almost none of these stereotypes, apart from the Georgian house he and his family eventually inhabited at the heart of industrial Preston, his birthplace. This 'makers' town was to be the place he would found BDP, setting it up in a disused biscuit factory that he and colleagues converted into the first burolandschaft office in the UK.

The first interdisciplinary studio of BDP. The burolandschaft conversion of the Vernon Street biscuit factory, Preston 1968.

I gained a further insight into the culture and direction of the early BDP during a recent meeting with three Prestonians who like many others followed Grenfell Baines, dedicating their lives to the work and culture of the practice. Grenfell Baines' widow Milena, who arrived in Preston after being evacuated from Czechoslovakia just before it was occupied by Nazi Germany, still lives in their house just by Avenham Park. On the outside, it's a handsome and minimal 1830s house, one of those built by industrialists for themselves when the town was convulsed by the industrial revolution, but still confident enough to sit in the centre rather than in some distant rural outpost. Inside, much of the original Georgiana has been stripped out, to be replaced with enough mid-century modern furnishings to make any Georgian conservationist have a coronary, with elegant but not remotely traditionalist clocks and dressers in a beautifully detailed wood. Milena remembers someone who was a 'great believer in modernism', not out of imposing something alien upon the industrial proletariat - because he grew up as part of it.

George Baines ('Grenfell' was his mother's maiden name) was the son of Methodist parents, living in the centre of Preston; his Dad worked on the railways. Milena recalls that, despite passing the exams, he never made it to grammar school, because 'his parents couldn't afford the uniform he had to go to work when he was 14, and studied at night. He got a job working as a draughtsman for a surveyor, and on being told by someone impressed with his drawings that he should become an architect, he replied 'what's an architect?' He would later be the first student to get a scholarship from Preston Council, to study at Manchester University, and then practise with Bolton firm Bradshaw, Gass and Hope - he was largely responsible for the detailing of Bolton Town Hall, being the only one who could do logarithms. His early work in the local area was eclectic, ranging from a Mock Tudor bungalow to an extraordinarily confident Aalto-esque interior for Preston's Stanley Arms Hotel. After going into private practice, Grenfell Baines and Hargreaves' break came with the Festival of Britain, where they were one of the few firms not based in London - their Power and Production Pavilion was an emblem of hard industrial modernity, in amongst this celebration of the early Welfare State and its informal, picturesque British modernism.

Right: George Grenfell Baines' early work in the Aalto-esque interior for Preston's Stanley Arms Hotel 1937.

Far right: The Power and Production Pavilion, Festival of Britain 1951 by Grenfell Baines and Hargreaves, the precursor practice of BDP. The only practice from the north of England to design a pavilion for the Festival.

The 1950s brought work on the new town programme - at Peterlee, where their unassuming plan replaced Lubetkin's original design, and Newton Aycliffe, along with other ventures like The Baines House, a simple and straightforward mild-modernist design that was the 'people's choice' in a 1956 competition in News Chronicle. Yet these designs were perhaps not really the point of his work - that was the collectivist politics that would lead to the establishment of BDP. He evidently wasn't satisfied with architecture alone, and Milena claims that 'he said if he weren't an architect, he would like to have been to be a musician, a mathematician or a politician', and traces of the first two and a heavy dose of the third left their mark on his work. 'He was certainly a socialist', according to her, and 'BDP's were socialist principles.' But, she continues, 'he realised you can't all be completely equal because there's different abilities'. So in his socialist pragmatist way, he formed a practice structure referred to as a 'pyramid turned upside down'.

It's quite something to hear such ideas now, after a decade-long explosion of ego and inequality, exhibited by both clients and architects. Clearly, GG's socialism, and his belief that democracy should be at the heart of the organisation of BDP, had inspired people as much as his charisma. Milena remembers that 'George didn't want the standard between the cleaner and the top man to be so huge' as it invariably was and is; while as for the name, 'he felt that the firm should not have a personal name because there were so many talented architects in the firm'. In so doing, he went a step further than the Architects Collaborative or Architects Co-Partnership, by not using the word 'architect' at all in the firm's name - like the 1920s Germans who avoided the aesthete connotations of the word, 'Building' was the preferred nomenclature. This extended to the way the practice worked itself - from 1961 until 1997, BDP was essentially a Co-operative rather than a normal limited company. The Bauhaus was in the background of this, as so much else. Milena says 'his ideal was the Bauhaus - the different professions all under one roof'. John Gravell, an architect who worked with GG in Preston all his professional life points out one important difference - 'Gropius had artists with him, but GG went that step further and integrated the engineers and planners'. In this, BDP was closer to the ideas of Hannes Meyer than those of Gropius directly.

The Early Works

'The pierced iron teapot stand over which I laboured as a schoolboy was, in my mother's eyes and mine, a beautiful piece of work. Even though the teapot occasionally fell off it our enthusiasm for the visual effect was scarcely damped. Here function was quite wrongly at a discount, but as emotion clouded judgement the balance between utility and aesthetics was, like the teapot, temporarily upset'.

George Grenfell Baines,
The Human Element in Planning, 1951.

Just round the corner from Milena, lives Keith Scott, an architect and planner and one of GG's early followers. Keith, a former BDP chairman, was also born and brought up in Preston and came from similar working class roots. Scott isn't particularly touched by nostalgia for the post-war era of architecture. He describes the dilemma of developing our traumatised cities, where the building stock was both poor and severely damaged by war. 'We had to produce a new building stock very quickly, so there was a need for rapid response and cheap methods of building that unfortunately resulted in a lot of shoddy architecture'. Yet this isn't quite the whole story. He points proudly to the Sandown Court tower blocks, two geometrically complex high-rises in the inner city, for which he led the design at BDP, but says 'they were built incredibly quickly, and never properly managed.' After years of neglect, though, in the last decade they became more prestigious, with the council selling off both blocks to a private developer. 'The interesting thing', Scott says, 'is that they work now they've been sold to private buyers. My son and I have bought one of the top floor flats'. It's a familiar story, over the last few years - the claim that modernism can work, if tailored to a rather more exclusive clientèle. And while the towers still stand as proudly and futuristically as they ever did, the lower blocks around were refurbished to be 'in keeping' with the surrounding Victorian housing.

For all that, Scott is clearly still deeply sympathetic to the ideas of architectural and social collectivity that infused BDP in the 1960s - not least because they allowed more freedom for the individual than more hierarchical firms would. 'I was a great believer in sharing, and everything GG did was based on sharing', and for that the hierarchy of architect over engineer, planner and sociologist was to be discarded - 'we all felt we needed to get all the professions working together.' In the practice itself, this made itself known through the design seminars, where partners would show their work to the group, 'and everyone said what they wanted - and I was keen on this, as you were still completely free to discount all that advice. Although you're a fool if you do.' In this, particular architectural tastes and sympathies were almost unimportant. He led the design of the Scarborough High School for Boys, which GG was not fully at one with, considering it too restless. Both men loved music and Grenfell Baines referred to it as being 'too much like Shostakovich'.

Here, the sharp, angular shopping centre that was designed in Blackburn is an example of quintessentially 1960s comprehensive redevelopment.

41

Scott reflected on the pressure GG put on him over the design, without ever instructing him to change it' something his egalitarian outlook could never bring him to do. Although it was not to his particular taste, he could tell it was a valid design'.

John Gravell, who worked as project architect for the Preston Bus Station, describes one crucial aspect of the collective culture - the individual designers at the time had great freedom. The stylistic multiplicity was he says, the consequence of 'there being many different architects in BDP', but also of the functionalist culture in which unexpected, unpredictable interactions between the client, the design team and the different disciplines formed the main dynamic of the practice. I ask Scott if there was a deliberate decision in the partnership to change course in the late 1970s - a change reflected in the buildings where he was directly involved. Here, the sharp, angular shopping centre in Blackburn, designed by an interdisciplinary team led by architect Bill White, is an example of the quintessentially 1960s comprehensive redevelopment that gave way to the highly decorative and apparently contextual postmodernism of the Ealing Broadway Centre. Scott is undisturbed by the change, indicated by the display of photographs of both projects mounted on the walls of his study. He says that in both cases, 'I don't think anything to do with style entered my head. I've never been one to be held back by stylistic reservations'. Both, he insists 'were dictated by the particular concerns of the site and the client' going on to talk about 'the essence of the streets' and 'the ethos of the place'.

Curiously, despite Baines' committed localism - even when BDP opened offices in London, Manchester and elsewhere, he never moved out of the town - Preston doesn't have as many works by BDP as might be expected. There's the two housing towers where Keith Scott was the principal designer, and the William Temple School, in a similarly restless and angular style to the 'Shostakovich' school and two buildings in the centre - a high-rise office block with a bristling ribbed concrete surface, and of course, the Preston Bus Station. Rumour has it that the lack of commissions from Preston Council had something to do with BDP's public objections to some of the 1960s' more destructive rebuildings of Preston, specifically the staid design of the new council offices next to the Park Hotel and demolition of the Public Halls. The north of England was prominent in the 1960s, both in post-war rebuilding and popular culture. Preston was represented here in the technological 'white heat' of the bus station in the centre of the town.

The bus station was initially the subject of some tension between BDP and the council; Milena Grenfell Baines, John Gravell and Keith Scott all agree that the partnership tried to explain to the council that the bus station was in the wrong place, and should be nearer to the main train station to the south. Scott believes the bus station is misconceived, although he would defend it against the traditionalists. He insists however that it is 'a standard multi-storey, with unique design for floor slab and a very elegant form. Functionally it has a number of flaws and I personally would be for pulling it down and putting it where it belongs'. It's an argument for architecture based on pure functionality, and in that it's very 1960s. The building itself is undoubtedly the most dramatic and unique piece of pure architecture in Preston, a swooping, fearless and highly dramatic monument to transport placed in the most unprepossessing setting on the ring-road.

The individual architect's freedom is demonstrated here, with lead designer Keith Ingham being specifically credited for the project as 'Keith Ingham and Building Design Partnership', and Milena Grenfell Baines remembers the consternation this originally caused. Yet the fact that such an original design was produced by an ostensibly faceless firm speaks for itself. Gravell, who was the project architect under Ingham taking me round the building's interior, points out the ideas that still survive here - the stunning elevation, the crisp original signage, which now competes with much clumsier later signs - and those that don't. The brief insisted on subways, and today people clamber over the fences and cross the bus aprons rather than use them. Ingham and BDP designed shops in the walkways and subways, in glass vitrines, with carpeting inside the bus station itself - Gravell says it was 'originally meant to be like a whole airport', as high-spec and luxurious as possible on a municipal budget. Yet within weeks the carpets were burnt, the seats were stolen and the glass in the shops in the subway was smashed. The shops were taken out after two years and never replaced; the white tiling there now is the replacement. Even then, the bus station won the Architectural Design Award 1969. Gravell, though, remembers that 'the police used to ring us up after each suicide asking for drawings. In a final irony, a 'Go Go Bus' sign in the bus station lost several of its letters, eventually ending up as 'GGB'. And despite an attempt to list it from English Heritage, the architects for the area's redevelopment as a new shopping area will, if it goes ahead, be BDP itself.

For all that, there's no doubt Preston Bus Station was an architectural triumph, and it is still held in very high esteem - a recent poll in the local press found it was the city's most popular building. Combined with BDP's equally dramatic, if slightly less distinguished office block opposite, it gives the city a raw, futuristic, instantly recognisable, robust and deeply northern skyline. Perhaps a more functionally successful example of this can be found on the other side of the Pennines in West Yorkshire.

Preston Bus Station. The design idea of bringing an airport style interchange, transforming the life and prospects of industrial northern cities.

The Halifax headquarters is the early BDP's most impressive riposte to the idea that a building designed by committee, or by an anonymous co-operative, can only be anonymous. Architecturally, the Halifax HQ is a thrilling collision of practically all of the ideas around at the time of its completion in the early 1970s. Brutalism, with the polygonal forms, typological complexity and rough material surfaces; Russian Constructivism, with its broken and angular forms; Miesian corporate modernism, with its sinister glamour, and smoked glass curtain wall; vernacular, with its local stone and its aggressive contextualism with the mills and mansions around it; and postmodernism, with part of the Building Society's original headquarters preserved under glass as a decontextualised object. Most of all, it feels an organic part of Halifax, of an architecturally and topographically dramatic industrial town. At the same time, here BDP connects itself with an earlier tradition of partnership and mutual assistance, by designing an emblem for one of the great 'mutuals' that became normal private

companies in the 1990s, the effects of which we are now familiar.

Scott says that the building's dramatic, eclectic design, largely the work of collective member Bill Pearson, was 'the spearhead of BDP being able to claim they were designers for all seasons'. 'I love the Halifax building', he continues, 'it's an amazing piece of architecture - worthy of standing in the pantheon of great architecture'. He then adds 'we've never been a cult, it was never part of our aim to be like the individual architects that emerged in the 1970s'. Here however, they could easily have become a cult, with this building clearly the equal of the early works by Rogers and Foster, except perhaps more valuable, because in its harsh physicality and its dark, Gothic presence, it is out of step with the stifling shiny optimism that high-tech helped create. So how did this extraordinary building occur? Scott in his typically matter-of-fact way, simply insists that 'it grew out of the site', an emanation of Halifax's existing presence.

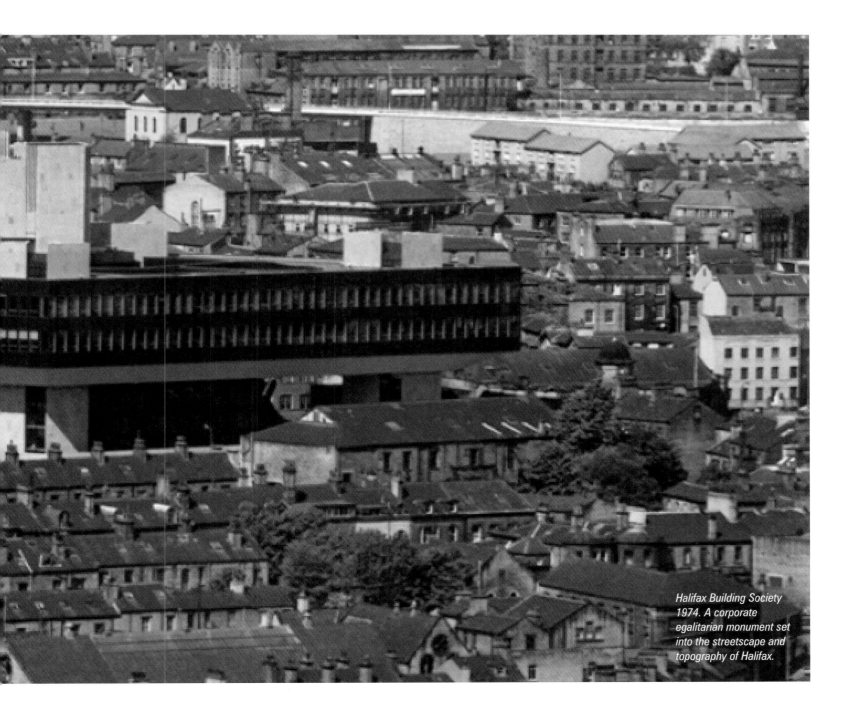

Halifax Building Society 1974. A corporate egalitarian monument set into the streetscape and topography of Halifax.

One of the later flagship projects, of the early period of BDP, was the headquarters for Imperial Chemical Industries in Wilton, Teeside, between Middlesbrough and Redcar, or rather between two ferociously powerful monuments to industrial strength, the Dorman Long works on one side and the British Steel (now Corus) complex on the other. Here at Wilton, any attempt to create something as sculptural as Halifax or Preston Bus Station would instantly have been overwhelmed by ICI's factory. This is a gigantic refinery, with monstrous concrete cooling towers and hundreds of chimneys and pipes - lit up at night, they are a metropolis all of their own, and local boy Ridley Scott claimed that they inspired the early sequences of Blade Runner. While Halifax could embody the industrial context, the Wilton Centre tried to leaven it instead. There's a redbrick industrial modernism to the buildings which is akin to James Stirling's 'red trilogy' (a language also seen at BDP's Haymarket Theatre in Leicester), and it sits low in the landscape, behind a large artificial lake. The interdisciplinary design team, led by Sid Tasker, has limited complexity in plan, creating a series of quiet interior courtyards reached via roads that pass underneath some of the main office blocks, in a manner Gropius pioneered with the Bauhaus building. Architectural dressing was limited to the public sculpture inside the courtyards, and the design of the canteen wing overlooking the lake, where a flurry of stepped forms contrasts with the linearity of the rest. In trying to create a serene landscape in such a strikingly industrial setting, the place sits somewhere between the brusque physicality of Brutalist campus universities and the incipient business and science parks, where ethereal high-tech or bloodless postmodern vernacular would be the aesthetic of choice. This 'landscape' of the interior had another meaning. As with its own office in Preston, it shows the influence on BDP of the post-war

German notion of burolandschaft, literally 'office landscape', intended to create an informal working environment without hierarchical organisation and a built embodiment of social peace and post-war consensus. This is something ICI were particularly keen on, with a programme of employee participation critically profiled in Theo Nicholls and Huw Beynon's melancholic book *Living with Capitalism*, published the year that the ICI Wilton Centre was completed.

Above: Flexible, open plan burolandschaft office space grouped around quiet interior courtyards.

ICI Headquarters, Wilton, Teesside 1974. Red brick industrial modernism, designed with a newly created landscape setting.

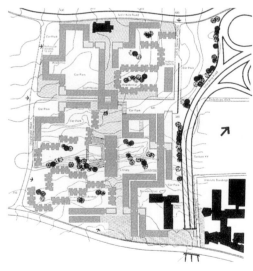

New universities for a new society. Bradford (above and left), Surrey (centre), Limerick (right). The universal space idea became the generator of the structured masterplans to this new generation of interdisciplinary academic institutions in the 1970s.

BDP's early projects found them literally building the 'progressive', high-tech Britain of the 1960s and 1970s, designing the new infrastructure of public health and education, or planning and redeveloping towns and cities, usually then in northern England. Designs for Leeds General Hospital and The Queen's Medical Centre, Nottingham got away from architecture's idea of a fixed, eternal monument through the use of flexible space, service floors and continuous maintenance. This universal space idea also influenced the designs for new universities, in Surrey, Bradford, Ulster and Limerick. At the Limerick Campus in the Republic of Ireland, BDP has over the past decade designed a new award winning campus on the north side of the river Shannon connected by pedestrian, cycle and road bridges to the earlier campus on the south bank. Each of these campus plans developed long term thinking linked to BDP's own focus on the collective and interdisciplinary design contribution. The architecture of Bradford University for instance, was deliberately elementary, readable and rationalist, with the processes of circulation and function inside dictating much of the external form; yet its low-rise blocks and tower were in a warm, brown aggregate which fitted well into the northern context, rather than trying to fight it. It's a stark contrast to current university buildings, often preoccupied with overt physical identity, and the pervasive attempt at iconic or landmark buildings.

The interest in regenerating and re-planning northern towns and cities obviously engaged many in BDP and as already described, they were often frustrated in their ambitions to reshape their hometown in Preston. An incipient conservation movement, given impetus by the publication in 1961 of Jane Jacobs' *The Death and Life of the Great American Cities* or, in the UK, the writings of Ian Nairn or J.M Richards' *The Functional Tradition*. These awakened many architects in industrial cities to the possibility of adapting and reusing the local 'functional tradition' - the powerful, if utilitarian old buildings and industrial districts.

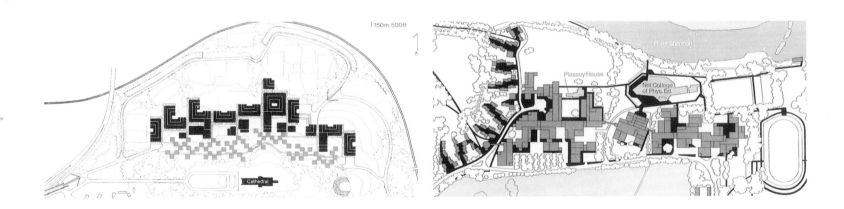

Appropriately, for a design collective that had colonised a disused biscuit factory for its design studio, adding to it an art gallery and recital hall for invited artists and musicians, BDP was at the forefront of this movement during the early 1970s. At Castlefields in Manchester it helped save the oldest railway buildings in the world, adapted and reused for a new Museum of Science and Industry, as well as facilities and studios for Granada TV. Also for Granada TV, Philip Hardwick's Dock Traffic Office at the Albert Dock, Liverpool was adapted for the news studio. Part of the Dock Warehouse buildings were also successfully converted for use as the Liverpool Maritime Museum.

At the same time, BDP was designing city centre shopping buildings - first modernist, as at Blackburn, followed later in the seventies by the townscape-influenced. These were exemplified initially by Durham Millburngate, the concept by Bill Pearson of traditional forms and rooftop topography was taken into a second stage by David Barnes and Adrian Jackson in BDP Manchester. The Lanes Carlisle also followed a neo-traditionalist route favoured by Keith Scott and David

Cash in Preston. Both projects, primarily shopping centres, won RIBA and Civic Trust Awards. Later at Ealing Broadway, BDP's Francis Roberts combined with Scott to design the richly detailed Arts and Crafts aesthetic to the shopping mall. The relationships and working knowledge BDP had formed with councils and developers in the modernist period stood it in good stead for the boom in shopping centre design that prevailed during the 1980s. Carlisle and Ealing in particular brought a mixture of uses, with libraries and housing departing from the typical modernist mall - after all, it had ironically been invented by another socialist, the Austrian architect Victor Gruen, to try and bring European community life into American suburbia. The American influenced combination of neo-vernacular, ostentatiously friendly forms and functional efficiency in these schemes proved to be hugely successful. The major political and economic shifts in early 1980s Britain marked the end of the beginning for BDP. Although it would continue to practise collectivity and sharing as a firm, *Living with Capitalism*, as the aforementioned book suggests, is precisely what it would be doing from then on.

*Above: The Lanes, Carlisle
1985. The design reconstitutes
the city streetscape, giving
way to a sequence of lanes
integrating shops, public library
and housing.*

*Below left: Castlefields, Manchester. Bringing new use and
new life to some of the oldest railway buildings in the world.*

*Below right: The Dock Traffic Office, Albert Dock, Liverpool
1846. Philip Hardwick's 'door stop' to the dock basins
adapted for use as the news studio for Granada TV.*

52

Durham Millburngate 1975. The setting as the starting point for the design. Regeneration of the city centre and riverside with towns and roof topography integrating with the historic cityscape.

Catalyst projects 1: They came from the North

During the half century since the formation of BDP, certain buildings and projects have proved crucial in moving the practice in new directions. Large or small, in every case they represent the start of a line of inquiry that enriches and informs other projects. Over time, they form not so much a family tree as an interlinking cluster diagram. Geography as well as chronology plays a part, and since BDP came out of the north west, we start with a key northern cluster. Important buildings here include Bradford University (1965-71) Preston Bus Station (1968-9) and the Halifax Building Society headquarters, completed in 1974. Education, transport, key corporate offices: these typologies were to wax and wane, but as with health and retail these remained important to the practice. Here we'll consider these catalyst buildings and what they led on to.

Two of them have landmark status, and all three are to do with northern civic pride, in an almost Victorian way. Preston, of course was BDP's home town and for many years its HQ office. The bus station/car park project first came into the Grenfell Baines group in 1959, pre-BDP: several iterations followed before the brief and the design crystallised. Client and designers were both building for the greater glory of Preston. So while bus stations are often ruthlessly utilitarian, not so here. In the hands of the BDP team, headed by Keith Ingham and (unusually, given the interdisciplinary ethic) working with engineers Ove Arup, these raw materials added up to a notable sculptural presence, a grand modern structure that could easily stand comparison with the industrial buildings of the city's past. At 560 feet or 171 metres long, it was an urban megastructure, a true groundscraper.

One particular design gesture ensured the building's fame: the curving, projecting shell-concrete balcony edges to the four car park levels. These served both to glorify a humdrum function, and to provide shelter to the bus passengers embarking and disembarking down below. What in other hands would have been a basic edge detail thus became the aesthetic driver of the whole building. Inside were bus company offices, lofty heated waiting rooms, shops, cafes. The photographs from the time show the building as space-age compared with the old-school Leyland buses pulled up against it, while its open-jointed white-tile end elevations spoke of the same kind of wipe-clean modernity as several of the new universities of the time. Everything was designed down to the last detail, including airport-style signage by the in-house BDP graphics team.

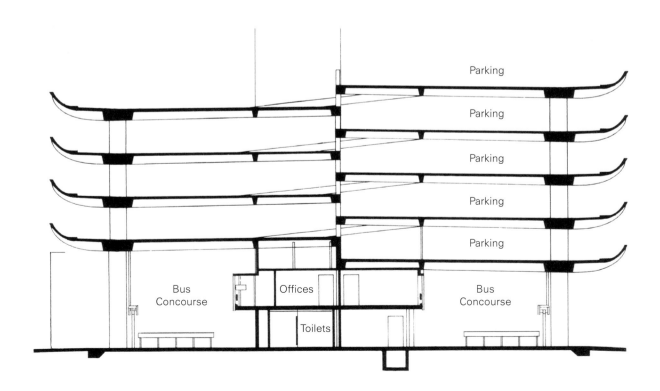

Opposite page: Preston Bus Station. Section showing the simple structure of car park above the bus concourse. It was the architecture of the

floor edges together with the treatment of the concourse space that created the memorable modernist dynamic

Above left: The airport style passenger concourse designed in detail right down to the graphics.

Above right: Architecture and structure intertwine to herald the arrival of modernity in one of the UK's oldest industrial cities.

It had no fewer than 80 departure gates - the result of combining into one building various previously dispersed terminals. Even so, you wonder if it really needed to be this big. Part of the replanning of the whole town centre, it managed to combine public and private transport - bus and car - at a time when the shift from one to the other was starting to accelerate. Pre-transport deregulation, it was designed for two main bus operators - one each side - with just eight bays at one end for the private sector. Thirty years later, with bus services privatised and atomised and car ownership near-universal, its future was in doubt. Forty years later -

the time of writing - its doom was sealed, with calls for it to be listed rejected, and government approval given for the £700m Tithebarn retail scheme which will replace it - ironically also involving BDP. Far too large for today's numbers of bus travellers, a perceived obstruction to the permeability of the city centre, with unfashionable pedestrian subway access, it was seen as time-expired. But for the purposes of this account, at the time it set a standard for other cities and other offices of BDP: while today it stands as a memory to a particular kind of progressive design ambition: that nothing was too good for the common people.

*One particular design gesture ensured the building's fame: the curving,
projecting shell-concrete balcony edges to the four car park levels.*

In line with that thinking, Bradford University was a classic 'plate glass university' of the period - as they were called to distinguish them from the previous wave of redbrick provincial universities. Designed and built at the same time as BDP's southern offices were laying out Surrey University in Guildford using system-building techniques, the Bradford example was, as befitted its mill town setting, an altogether craggier affair. The massive cast-concrete rooftop ping-pong table at one point gives the flavour: this was Brutalism with a twist. Instead of the curvilinear delicacy of the Preston Bus Station, here you got the homage to the right angle, the in-situ frame, the precast cladding panel - contrasted with brick and stained timber for the student residences. Bradford, always the poor relation of adjacent big-city Leeds with its long-established redbrick university, was playing catch-up, and allocated a dramatically sloping 32 acre valley site just outside the city's new ring road (another badge of civic pride at the time) for the universification of its former technical college.

The buildings that formed the core of this new university make the most of the site's intrinsic drama, tucking into the rising ground either side of a central pedestrian spine. Perhaps it borrows a little from the planning of Sir Basil Spence's topographically related Sussex University, but this is a much denser, tougher, urban variant, its technical credentials established by the first faculty building, for chemical engineering and nuclear science. A sequence of courtyards and covered routeways defined circulation. By the time BDP had contributed its last, communal, building in 1977 - the one with the concrete-slab ping-pong table - the aesthetic had softened just a little with yellow-brick cladding but was still openly industrial in feel. A university by northerners, for northerners.

Bradford University. The masterplan makes the most of the site's intrinsic drama, tucking into the slope on either side of the pedestrian movement spine.

A sequence of courtyards and covered walkways defines the student experience with an architecture that has an openly industrial feel.

Our final core example in this mill town triumvirate is one of the great overlooked corporate offices of the early 1970s: the Halifax Building Society headquarters. Once impeccably maintained, since the banking crisis of 2008 and the near-collapse of the outfit by then known as HBOS (Halifax Bank of Scotland) it has now become peripheral offices for the Lloyds banking group. But back in the days when the Halifax was the

nation's largest mutual building society, mortgage and savings based, with no 'casino' banking operations, the building was built to be as powerful as the organisation itself, and was used in its marketing material. The organisation's previously scattered offices were to be brought together: 18 months were spent refining the brief. Much research was done into office working patterns.

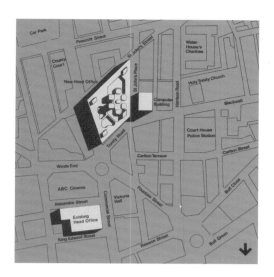

The Halifax Building Society Headquarters. The building was a striking new city block dedicated to this important town. It became as much of a civic presence of this great 20ᵗʰ century institution as the mills were in the 19ᵗʰ century. This time rather than being rooted in the earth it was thoroughly modern, seemingly floating in the townscape.

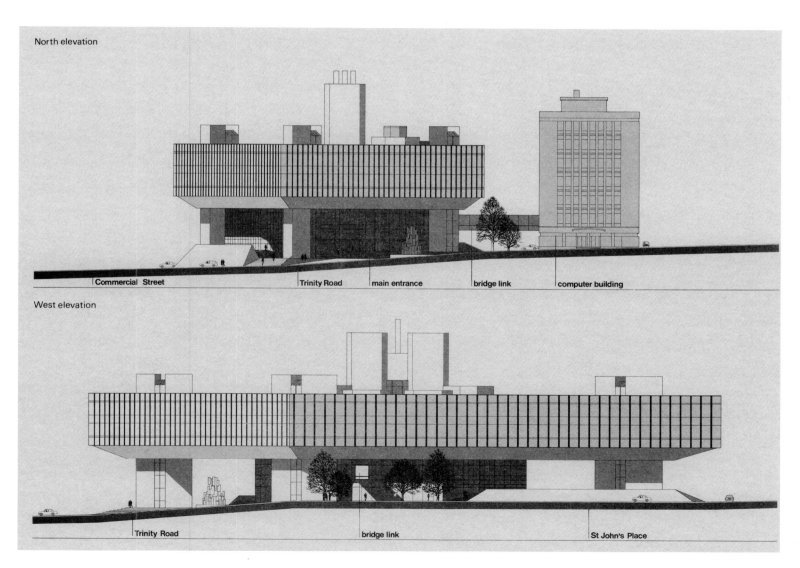

North elevation

Commercial Street | Trinity Road | main entrance | bridge link | computer building

West elevation

Trinity Road | bridge link | St John's Place

Rhomboidal on plan, its key move in elevation was to separate the served and servant spaces vertically and emphatically, raising the main two storeys of offices and meeting rooms in a two-storey band of Miesian curtain-walling placed high on four corner staircase towers, which follow the same rhomboidal geometry as the building's grid. The structural engineering required for this, borrowing from bridge technology, was more than a little adventurous for the building industry of the time. One of these two floors is the vast (4,600 sq m) burolandschaft general office: above, perimeter cellular offices, boardroom and meeting rooms open out onto landscaped rooftop water courts. The early 1970s oil crisis coincided with construction, and the building's full air conditioning attracted criticism from ecological quarters. However a basic heat recovery system was installed.

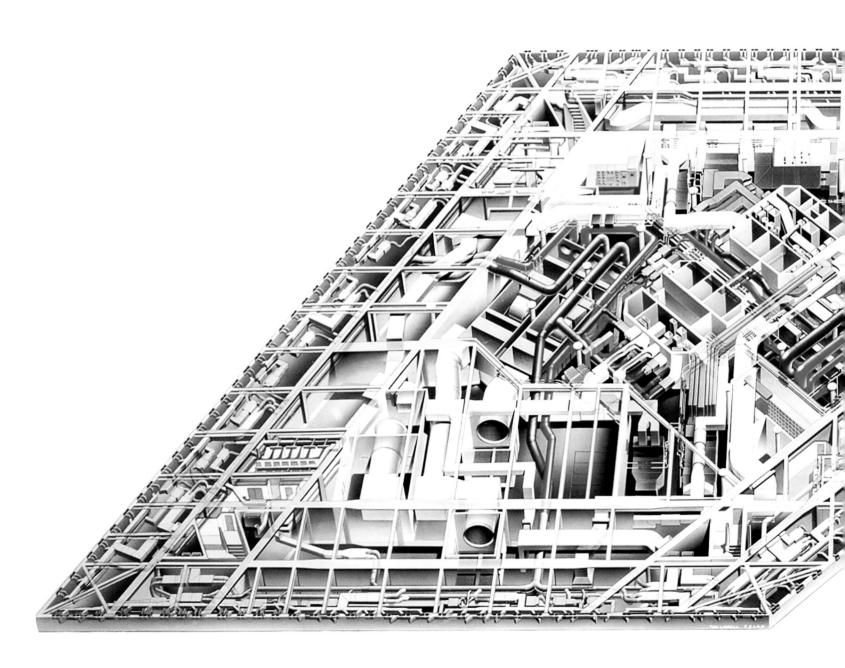

Co-ordinating structure and environmental engineering with the architecture and interior character was the essence of the design for this ambitious HQ of the time. The interstitial floor - that is a complete floor - dedicated to technical servicing, freed up the rest of the building as a complete environment for the users, interrelating them with their surroundings and freeing up the roof space as a vital and active part of the townscape as in the great Victorian buildings.

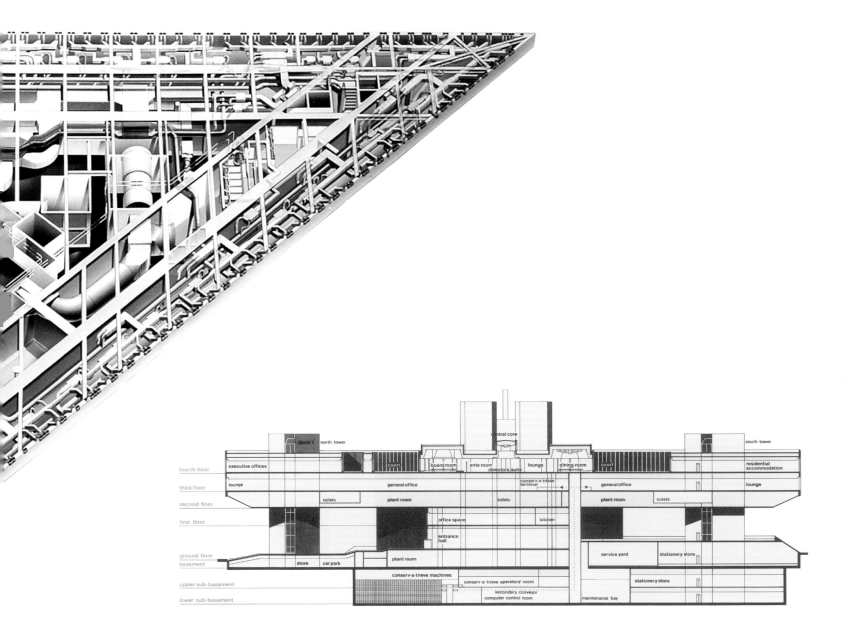

The design team explored the briefing process with the user groups to fully understand all their needs. It not only became a major piece of urban design and architecture, but also one of graphic and product design detailing everything down to each person's pencil drawer.

Each area was designed around its users, bringing the highest level of modern design to everyone who worked in the Halifax. The cornfield coloured carpet became a legend in the practice and a symbol of design altruism.

The home owner's deeds and their physical transfer throughout the building reflect the care for savers which formed the original ethos of the Halifax as one of the UK's great mutual societies.

Down below is a podium accessed via flights of steps from street level: and below the podium is, or was, a mighty undercroft for documents, including an automated 'Conserv-a-triev' store for title deeds, powered by early computers. These vital documents travelled vertically through a central service core to and from the general office. Intended to reflect the solidity and permanence of the institution as well as its importance as a big employer in this medium-sized town, the building is by today's standards astonishingly dominant from some views, but in its black and buff colour scheme also picked up on the colours of the surrounding townscape.

The architecture critic Ian Nairn called it 'a lifetime's achievement'. Peter Reyner Banham described it as 'Godzilla in Halifax', but approved, as did the main architecture magazines. Not everyone liked it, though. Stephen Gardiner in the Observer remarked: 'At one stroke Halifax has received a blow from which it can never recover'. The Yorkshire branch of the RIBA vociferously objected to its being given an RIBA award, but were overruled. This was, said the influential architect and taste-maker Sir Hugh Casson, a case of 'truly Victorian self-confidence'. However the design team led by Bill Pearson, with Richard Saxon

and engineer John Ellis, was sufficiently miffed by the negative reviews to write a lengthy response. 'It is a bold building for a bold client', they pointed out. 'We are encouraged by the fervour of public interest and response, both pro and anti. People either love or hate the thing, which is surely better than the non-reaction to a safe design'. It was, they said, 'the equivalent of the visual and social role of a minster in a medieval town'.

Forty years on, its original client long lost through demutualisation, industry mergers and the 2008 banking crisis, it still retains its visceral power. Owen Hatherley, shadowing Nairn in his polemical 2010 book *A Guide to the New Ruins of Great Britain*, described it as 'Genuinely one of the most unbelievable postwar buildings in the country…to call it dominant would be an understatement, the way it juts out across a Victorian street, but it also harmonises chromatically with Halifax's Yorkshire stone, brown and coal-stained black'. For him - as with Richard Rogers' later Lloyd's of London building - this was Leftist architecture, related to Russian Constructivism, pressed into the service of capitalism. It also anticipates the ground plane/elevated structure dialectic that was to obsess progressive architects such as Zaha Hadid at the end of the 20th century and beyond.

The Halifax building was, then, a game-changer for BDP. Big, corporate, radical - dare one say iconic - it showed that the firm could compete at the highest level, on an interdisciplinary basis, on innovatory buildings. This was indeed a fruitful period: a similarly rigorous geometry was deployed, for instance, in the otherwise more conventional redbrick industrial campus for ICI Petrochemicals in Wilton, Teesside, completed in 1975. Its rural background was the very opposite of the tightly urban Halifax HQ. Its multiple-courtyard cellular layout, contrasting informal social hub and landscaped lakeside setting deliberately gave it very much the appearance of a new university, with potential for easy expansion. It led onto a number of later commissions across the country for ICI, and today it has become home to dozens of smaller businesses. And, interestingly, a branch of Teesside University.

ICI Petrochemicals Headquarters, Wilton, Teesside.
The redbrick industrial campus stretches out to create
a new landscape and built environment akin to the
new universities of the 1970s and a counterpoint to
the engineering of the petrochemical processes.

It was sometimes an uphill battle to build. The Lisbon HQ of the Banco Espirito Santo e Comercial (BES), with its strong gridded brise-soleil façade, for instance, took from 1971 to 1975, delayed during building by the little matter of the Portuguese revolution: at one point the design team, led by Bill Jack, had to negotiate a cordon of tanks to get to meet its somewhat beleaguered clients. There was, however, an ultimate HQ building that got away around this time, and like the BES, it came from the London office rather than the northern ones. The

United Nations building and conference centre in Vienna won in a two-stage competition against the cream of international architects in 1969 - only to become mired in politics and never built. This would have been a startling megastructure, of highly sculptural extruded-ziggurat form, positively sci-fi in appearance. It had the potential to be one of the great European buildings of the period. 16 storeys high, 370m long by 160m wide, it would have contained a remarkable central hall. Had it been built, the practice might well have done a great deal more overseas

Above: The Banco Espirito Santo e Comercial Headquarters, Lisbon. A dignified city block of a building set on the city's most important boulevard.

work, much sooner. As it was, the competition win was a huge morale-booster, especially for BDP's interdisciplinary design team led by architects Bob Smart and David Rock.

What this intriguing flourishing of buildings and projects tells us is the level BDP had got to in the first decade of its existence: from a northern group practice with a tiny London outpost to a firm that could handle projects at all scales and levels of ambition, nationally and internationally. But all this was to lead in two very different directions.

Below: The United Nations Building, Vienna. This competition winning accessible monument, conceived as a sculptural ziggurat on the island overlooking Vienna, proved too radical to be realised.

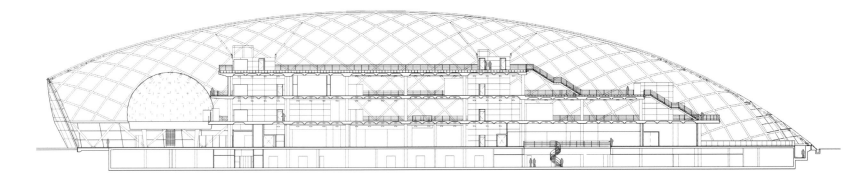

One direction was the landmark (signature, icon, monumentalist) building: that strand was to resurface at the end of the century. For instance, a competition winning team from BDP Glasgow led by Andy McCrory, with Colin Allan and Gareth Maguire, created a new city landmark with the titanium-clad forms of the Glasgow Science Centre, in design terms one of the best of the lottery-funded Millennium projects. This led to a further competition winning scheme from the Glasgow studio, with the Perth Concert Hall designed by Sandy Fergusson, with Angus Kerr, Bruce Kennedy and director of acoustics Duncan Templeton. Further competition winning schemes, at the city scale, included a number of city block office buildings as part of a BDP masterplan in The Broomielaw on Glasgow's riverside. Led by the same architect Graham McClements, the later crescent shaped headquarters building for Scottish Widows in Edinburgh takes the urban block further as a new corporate gateway to the west of the city centre.

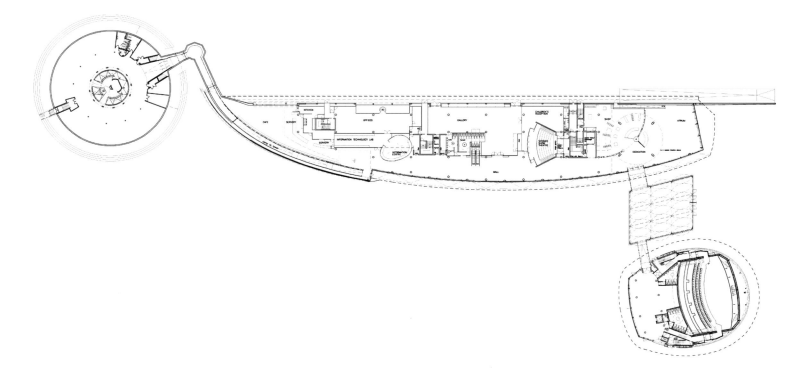

Above: Glasgow Science Centre. Titanium clad technoshell forms regenerate the riverside with a new place for the city.

Right: A new city gateway dedicated to inspiring the city's young people, and inspiring others who are dedicated to science.

TOGETHER
WE FLY HIGHER.

Who will dream up the designs of tomorrow?

Today's schoolchildren, of course. That's why

Boeing and the Royal Aeronautical Society

created the 'Schools Build a Plane Challenge'.

The first aircraft is scheduled to premiere at the

2010 Farnborough Air Show. And the inspired

engineers of the future will fly higher together.

Discover more at boeing.co.uk/together

A science building for the city that attracts families and children to discover the wonder and enjoyment of science.

The thin section of stacked exhibition platforms within the titanium shell commands a city scale window over the river Clyde. A civic beacon by day and by night.

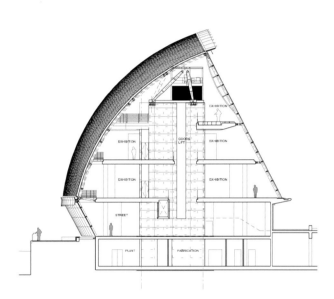

In terms of landmark corporate office complexes, look no further than the 1998 Opel car HQ in Rüsselsheim, Frankfurt. The interdisciplinary design, led by Richard Saxon and Tim Williams with engineers Andrew Swain-Smith and Farah Jahanpour, arguably contains some of the planning ideas of the UN building, albeit in much less outré form. A calmer aesthetic had developed by the time of the 2006 Roche HQ in Welwyn in the UK, in which Tim Williams with Mark Bax, Chris Langston and interior designer Martin Cook, engineers James Warne and Trevor Butler, brought an appropriately Swiss sense of clean, minimal detailing overlaid on a highly sustainable concept for the famous Swiss pharmaceuticals giant.

Top left: Perth Concert Hall. A new civic building regenerating an area at the heart of the city. Its versatile 1200 seat auditorium which accommodates activities ranging from orchestral concerts, drama, conference, sport and recreation, has become an exemplar of flexibility for performance spaces in the UK.

Right: The Broomielaw, Glasgow. The masterplan ties into the Glasgow grid, regenerating this area along the river Clyde. The new office quarter, sets modernist civic architecture to compliment that of the Victorians.

Left: Scottish Widows Headquarters, Edinburgh. The modern crescent forms of the new headquarter building create a new civic gateway to the west of the city centre.

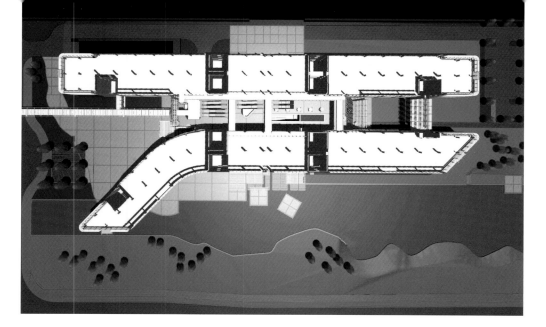

Opel Headquarters, Rüsselsheim, Frankfurt. The headquarters designed as a people's street draws the people in the company together in a new administrative gateway, adjacent to the car manufacturing areas.

Opel Car Museum, Rüsselsheim, Frankfurt. Technological detailing linked to mood architecture forms an atmospheric backdrop for the car show.

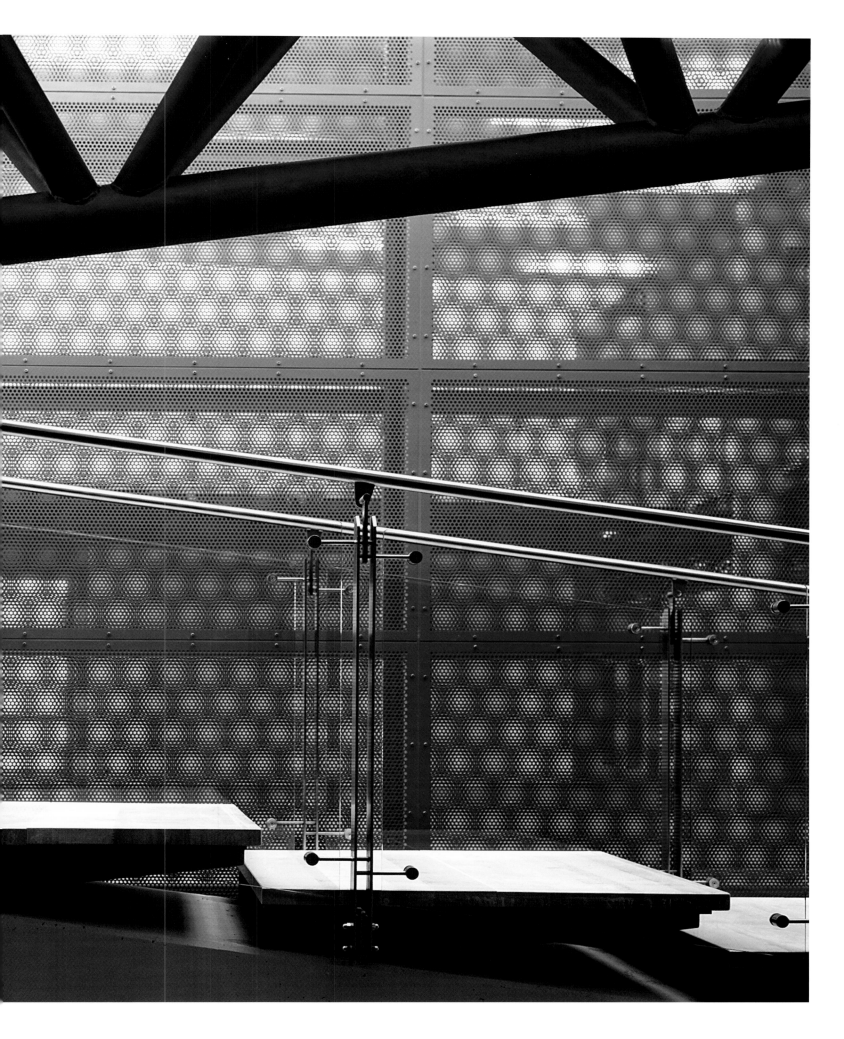

Roche Headquarters, Welwyn Garden City, Hertfordshire. Clean architectural lines and an interior character designed as an office street and garden courtyards create a simple identity with outstanding sustainable credentials.

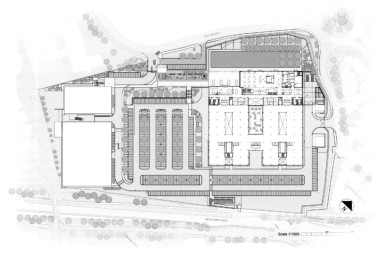

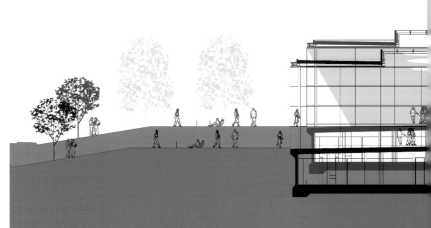

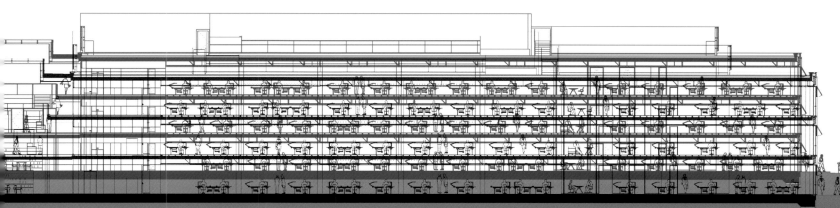

But there was another strand which emerged from these northern catalyst buildings, paradoxically one that was all to do with context and reuse, rather than the tabula rasa building. If Halifax had a Victorian mill-owner's loud and proud attitude to context, then Durham's competition-winning Millburngate Centre was its exact opposite - and strangely, led by the same architect and design leader: brick and slate, jumbled roofs, consciously Romantic, positively deferential. This being the start of the 1970s, it was vernacular in spirit rather than postmodern, skilfully deploying its devices to break down the bulk of what was then, for this small and lovely city, a biggish shopping mall with residential attached. It was designed such that its fifth elevation - its roofscape - made visual sense when viewed from the Norman castle and cathedral perched high above. Suddenly, BDP was winning awards from the conservation sector. While it was to become noted for large-scale shopping centres in the 1980s, such relatively small, contextual exercises continued, as the Lanes centre in Carlisle of the early 1980s demonstrates. Including a public library, and replicating under cover the historic alleyways of the city, it was successful in concealing its bulk in the historic fabric - though not all took kindly to what some saw as its pastiche jumbled main street frontage of reconstructed house fronts. A bit harsh, since the whole idea was to be inconspicuous. At least - again - it wasn't PoMo, though BDP along with many others was to dabble briefly in that style later: the mid to late 1980s Ealing Broadway Centre with its big recycled slate roofs and redbrick lift-tower turrets is the touchstone there.

Above: Ealing Broadway, London. A new vernacular streetscape approach to the extension of shopping and commerce on one of London's important high streets.

Right: The Lanes, Carlisle. The new arcaded lanes off the high street seamlessly bring new shopping, housing and a public library to the city.

The Royal Opera House, Covent Garden, London. Masterplan and Adaptation. The Floral Hall, adapted as the entrance and hospitality foyer, creates a new/old sense of drama between the acts.

A new movement - the testing of alternatives to both unalloyed modernism and comprehensive clearance - was taking hold, first seen in the alternative reuse suggested for Liverpool's Albert Dock. The project did not materialise, but other work in the Albert Dock did, such as the first designs for the Liverpool Maritime Museum and the mid 1980s restoration of the Dock Traffic Office as the city's centre for Granada Television. A continuing expertise in preservation and enlightened reuse came out of this, which was eventually to feed into such projects as the Royal Opera House and Royal Albert Hall radical refurbishment in London. These two projects were carried forward into realisation by Charles Broughton and Tim Leach on the Opera House and a wave of profession leaders on the Royal Albert Hall; architects Nick Terry and Martin Ward, engineers Michelle McDowell, Bob Spittle and Steve Runicles with costs and project planning by Peter Snape and Andrew Whitehurst. BDP was advancing on a number of heritage fronts around the firm, with the reshaping of Kelvingrove Art Gallery, Glasgow by Angus Kerr and Ken Moth, major adaptation for King's College London at Somerset House, the revitalisation of Chatham Historic Dockyard, both led by Tim Leach and still those northern warehouses boldly represented by Navigation Warehouse, Wakefield, again by Ken Moth.

The Royal Albert Hall Masterplan and Refurbishment. The reshaping of the world famous performance hall was carried out between 1996 and 2005 without losing a single performance.

The Royal Albert Hall, London, Masterplan. The creation of a subterranean back of house, reshaping of the auditorium, creation of new hospitality areas and a new entrance building retain the iconic character of the place while providing flexibility and increasing comfort levels for international performance from music to tennis.

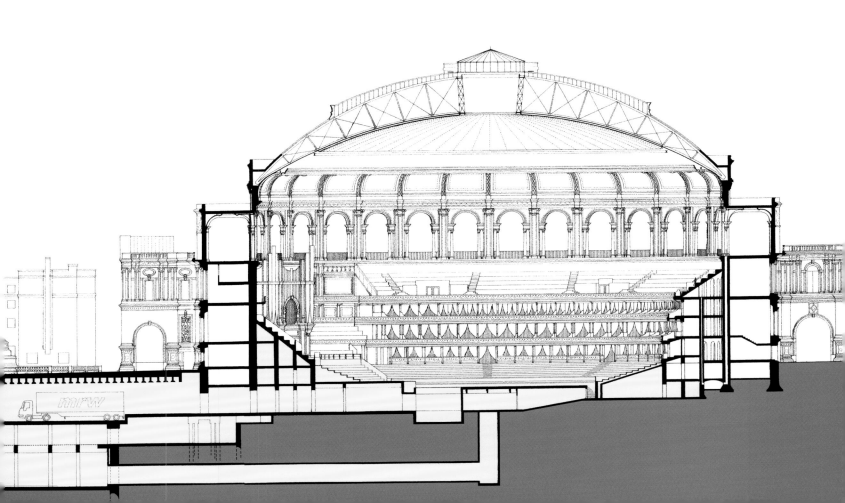

Kelvingrove Art Gallery and Museum, Glasgow. Seamless, spatial reshaping of galleries and redundant areas have created 30 % more space and 50 % more exhibits, without extending one of the most loved buildings in Scotland.

Catalyst projects 2: the Learning Curve

Hampden Gurney Primary School, Westminster, London. Concept section of the vertical school. Covered playdecks enjoy the south light with glare free learning in the north facing classrooms. The school hall is at the bottom and a pupils' technology garden on the top.

One of BDP's smallest projects was the primary school at Hampden Gurney in London's Marylebone. This was one of those projects that hung around the studio for quite some time. A good original idea - a reinvention of the 19th century urban primary school, like the London Board Schools, this time with the playgrounds in the sky - it was the kind of scheme, depending on a property deal for funding, that could so easily have remained on paper. But it didn't. Eventually, after a three and a half year struggle with the planners and education department, it was built. When I reviewed it for *The Sunday Times* in 2001, I was clear what was going on: this was one of a small crop of 'outrageously original' new schools then emerging, at both primary and secondary level. Why stick to the conventional model, I pondered, where the school is like a low edge-of-town supermarket, surrounded by playgrounds rather than car parks? Why not think differently - in this case something that more closely resembled a beehive?

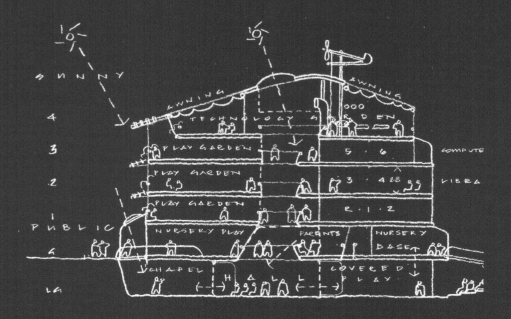

Indeed, Hampden Gurney led on to an exemplar design study for the Department of Education specifically called the 'Beehive School' which imagined the concept scaled up to allow a bigger primary school to be built on a confined site. Again, this made it from concept to reality in the form of a major secondary school for the Bridge Academy, Hackney in 2008, by which time BDP was getting very heavily involved in what may come to be seen as a short-lived golden age of state school renewal. The unconventional design of Hampden Gurney stemmed from an invited competition judged by the chairman of the school trustees. The winning design was led by Tony McGuirk with Helen Groves and Gareth Jones who developed the vertical layers of classroom and playdeck hung off a highly unusual bowspring top-hung structure designed by engineer Farahmand

Jahanpour, so allowing the large column-free school hall and a part-covered playground to occupy the basement.

It was driven by this Church of England school's very pragmatic funding strategy: to pay for the new school by building housing for sale on part of the site. Previously this had been a Second World War bombsite with a 1950s school parked on it, but prior to that it formed the end of a city block with houses, school and church. The presence of the existing school obviously reduced the area available, but the vertical stacking meant no loss of amenity. On the contrary: with the various ages of pupil rising from youngest to oldest as you go up, each with its own playdeck or lower ground playground, the eternal problem of older children knocking over younger ones simply vanished. A bilateral split between the playdecks (and rooftop technology

Hampden Gurney School.
Below left: The plan showing the school and housing completing the urban block of the street grid in Marylebone, Westminster, London.

Below right: A typical plan of classrooms and playdecks. Pupils play with their own age groups.

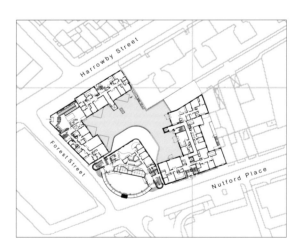

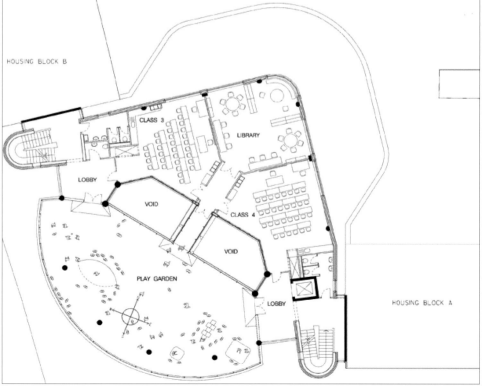

garden) at the front and the classrooms at the back is provided by a narrow full-height atrium crossed by access bridges - doing away with old style corridors.

Looking at the drawings today, it is as original as ever, one of the more unusual sets of plans, sections and elevations you are likely to encounter. But this relatively small building served to confirm what was becoming apparent to outside observers such as me: after the years of aesthetic uncertainty in the 1980s, BDP had rediscovered its modernist design mojo. There always have to be generational shifts within design firms - very often hastened by economic downturns - and the big purge of the early 1990s which led to so many new practices being formed, happened also to coincide with the retirement of a whole generation of partners who had helped build the organisation up in the first place. It was

a time for fresh thinking as one-time juniors rose through the ranks to take over the controls. Just as the Halifax HQ formed a benchmark in the hard-edged early 1970s, so in the 1990s, coming out of recession, an equally radical shift took place in the form of a return to humanist-inspired Scandinavian modernism. Given that the firm's founder, George Grenfell Baines, channelled Aalto in his early solo work in the late 1930s, this was a return to a different set of roots. The key project to consider in this context is the University of Sunderland. The first of three phases built over a 10-year programme was completed in 1994. The wholly interdisciplinary project was led by Tony McGuirk with Chris Harding, interior designer Jack Hobbs, lighting designer Barrie Wilde, engineer Andrew Swain-Smith, landscape architect Nick Edwards and project and cost planning by Peter Snape and Andrew Whitehurst.

Below: Hampden Gurney School. Section through the vertical school and housing showing the new urban city block with the school as the public cornerpiece.

Hampden Gurney School. Right: Beacon School. Playdecks and classrooms at every level of learning. Children grow up the school with nursery at ground and 11 year olds on top.

Below: A school without corridors. The central light and air space visually links the pupils on their playdecks and in their classrooms to the central hall below.

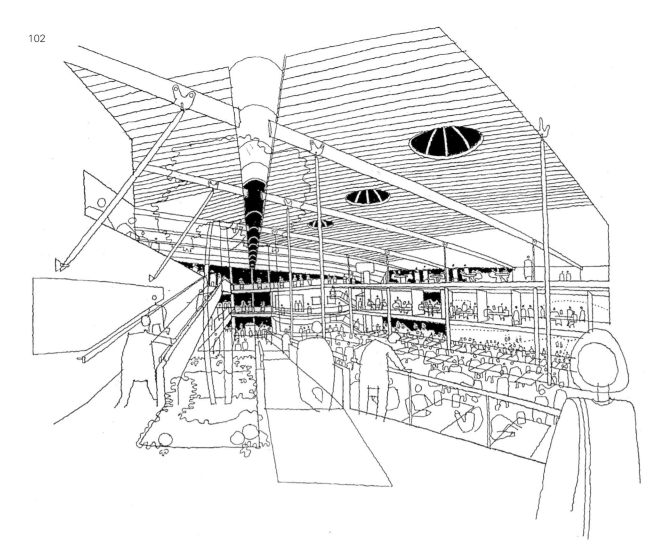

Left: University of Sunderland concept sketch of the Informatics and Computing Centre, showing the stepped computing hall.

Below: Section through the campus showing buildings acting as through routes taking students from the upper slope to the water's edge.

This was a time of great formal experimentation in British architecture in the aftermath of postmodernism: at the same time, for instance, Will Alsop was completing his breakthrough building, the Hôtel du Département or 'Grand Bleu' in Marseilles. There was a desire among architects at this time to pull apart the elements of a building complex, expressing each function individually, to re-examine architecture's very operating system. Alsop's was vertically-stacked and glossy: Sunderland spread horizontally along the terrain but by no means chaotically, mixing rough and smooth finishes, down its postindustrial

site to the river Wear. It was and is an academic village, a grouping that acknowledges the picturesque, the organic and the humanist in a way that the sternly rationalist campuses of the practice's early years did not (but that the vernacular-inspired Millburngate Centre in Durham certainly did). It has a fascination with materiality, especially in this case rough-sawn timber. Another telling parallel from the period is the curvaceously rough-hewn 1992 Fountains Abbey Visitor Centre in Yorkshire by Edward Cullinan, which nonchalantly mixed modernism with old-time craft skills.

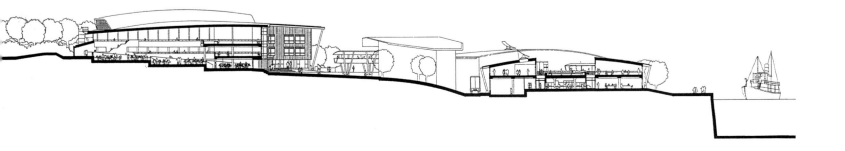

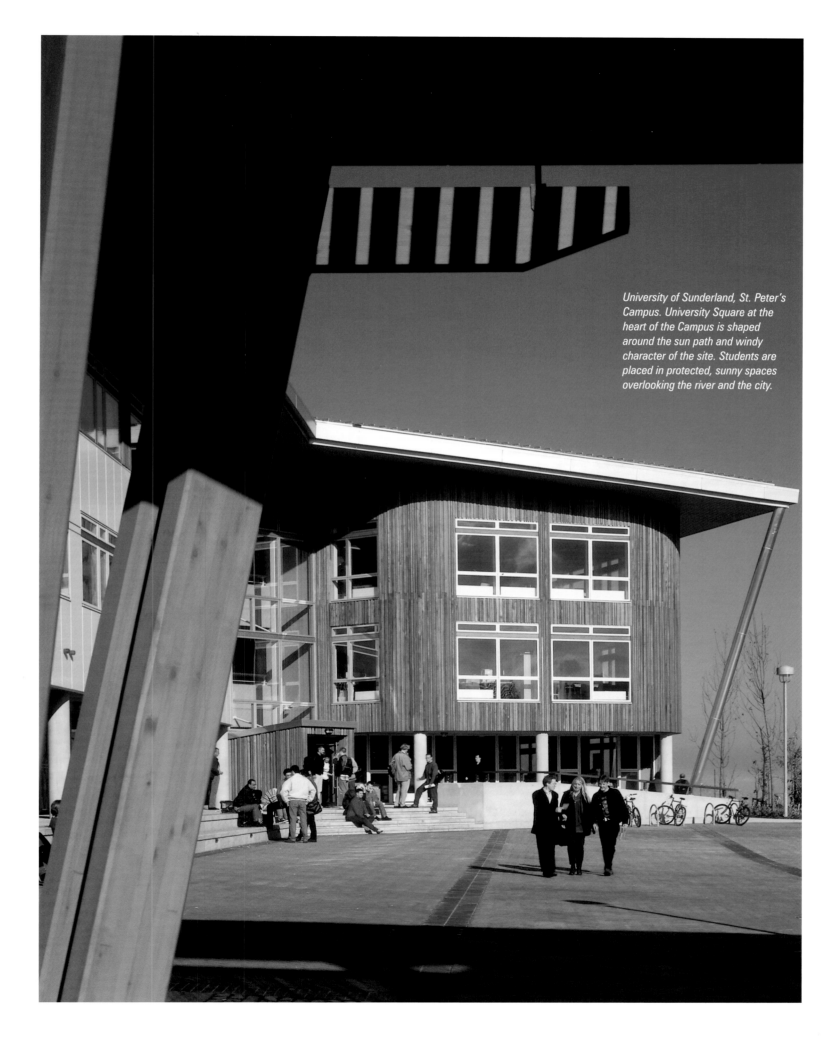

University of Sunderland, St. Peter's Campus. University Square at the heart of the Campus is shaped around the sun path and windy character of the site. Students are placed in protected, sunny spaces overlooking the river and the city.

Above: University of Sunderland, St Peter's Campus. The Informatics and Computing Centre. Electronic learning terraces step down the sloping site to river, sun and view.

Right: The Reading Room. An organic and human scale space dedicated to silent learning in a digital interactive campus.

*Regenerating
Sunderland's industrial
riverside. The disused
shipyard is given a new
life as a new centre of
learning.*

The heroes were changing: this kind of design was from what Colin St John Wilson, academic and architect of the British Library, called 'the alternative tradition of modern architecture'. However, at Sunderland Aalto was filtered through the later work of Anglo-Swedish architect Ralph Erskine, with whom Tony McGuirk had worked after graduating on another notable project in the north east of England, the now-listed Byker development in Newcastle-upon-Tyne. Like Byker, Sunderland University gave focus to an area which was, through large-scale clearances, in danger of losing its identity.

*Marlowe Academy,
Ramsgate, Kent. Galleries to
teaching space combine with
the student heartspace and
performance centre to create
the school as theatre.*

Hampden Gurney School built on the impact of the earlier Sunderland University, and got to the Stirling Prize shortlist, but the two projects - relatively loose and informal, the other ultra-compact - were aspects of the same research into the internal connections of places of learning. From there one looks to the embracing arms of Bridge Academy by architect Tony McGuirk, Keith Papa and Keith Watson, along with engineers Oliver Plunkett, James Warne and lighting designer Laura Bayliss. Appropriately this vertical secondary school was built on the site of a former multi-level Board School, with its separate sports and performance buildings in a tight, linked complex. There are several others in the crop,

such as the 2006 award-winning Marlowe Academy in Kent led by Benedict Zucchi with Oliver Plunkett and Andrew Swain-Smith, with its great central space beneath a curving timber coffered roof and the sinuous Highbury Grove School by Wayne Head and Dominic Hook knitting into a leafy area of Islington, North London. The Devonshire Primary School in Blackpool of the same year as Marlowe was another product of the 'Beehive School' study from the Manchester studio's Gavin Elliott, Sue Emms and engineer Jonathan Pye, like Hampden Gurney incorporating stacked classrooms with attached playdecks and a rooftop garden - but in this case open to the community at large as well.

Bridge Academy, Hackney, London. The vertical secondary school forms a new beacon to the regeneration of the canalside setting, with central heartspace of student piazza, library and café restaurant.

Right: Bridge Academy, Hackney, London. A school without corridors. Galleries to teaching spaces with informal learning areas overlook the heartspace and out to the canalside neighbourhood.

Below: The Devonshire 'Beehive' School, Blackpool. Sunny playdecks look out over the town to its famous tower.

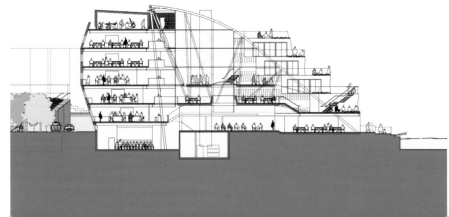

Right: Bridge Academy, Hackney, London. Section showing the 'hoop' structure that creates a column free centre to the school for students gathering and events.

*Bridge Academy,
Hackney, London.
The hoop structure
carries the heart of the
building and its learning
activities. The column
free student piazza and
restaurant sit below.*

The vertical urban school, music auditorium and sports centre as a regenerator of the canalside neighbourhood. All accommodated in an area smaller than the size of a football pitch.

This line of inquiry into school design continues on through the De Driemark Community School, Winterswijk, in the Netherlands, under construction at the time of writing. The London studio's Tony McGuirk and Murray Kerr collaborated with Marcel Seelen in the new Dutch studio on the design that brings together three existing schools into one location. It follows the pattern of a multi-level school with a heartspace which avoids corridors, and is shaped to shelter pupils and teachers from the prevailing winds. Like Bridge Academy, it will act as a spur to regeneration of a run-down area. In this case it is built on a former railway marshalling yard where a new cultural hub for Winterswijk is planned. The thinking has evolved: here for instance is a highly novel feature, a wooden-clad teaching hub hanging in the central heartspace. This will contain specialised teaching facilities, theatre and library.

De Driemark School, Winterswijk, the Netherlands. Three schools in one form a new public learning centre with sports and gymnastics hall regenerating the railway quarter of the city.

Opposite: Special subjects are set within a 'hanging basket' structure at the centre of the school with the public thoroughfare below.

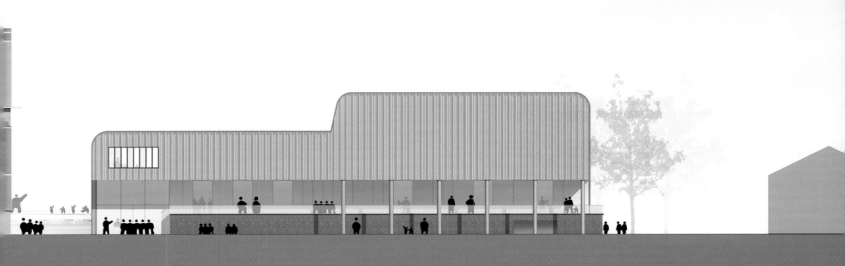

If Hampden Gurney School led on to several other such spin-offs, then so did the University of Sunderland in the higher education sector. This was less a case of refining a design prototype, more to do with the capabilities it demonstrated. So for instance the University of York Heslington East Campus masterplan places its buildings around climatically protective landscape courtyards leading to a main lakeside building, in the spirit of the original. The design of the first phase, interlinked masterplanners Tony McGuirk and Kathryn Tombling in the London studio with architects Stephen Hill and Richard McDowell in Sheffield with interior design and lighting by Katharine Blankley and Mark Ridler. The residential element, Goodricke College, is a community

of student accommodation in which the influence of Sunderland is clear. Elsewhere on the campus, the 2009 Berrick Saul research centre adopts a curving organic form - not only in contrast with the existing blocky buildings, but in order to weave around an important existing group of trees as part of Karen Howell's landscape strategy for the site.

The University of York, Heslington East Campus. A new lakeshore campus, with buildings and spaces designed around climate and the landscape setting.

Below: The interdisciplinary Hub Building. A window on the lakeshore interconnects inside and outside in a relaxed student experience.

Left: Goodricke College. Student living shaped around protective garden courtyards with buildings formed around the sunpath.

Below, left: The Hub Building. Overlooking the lake it forms a suntrap magnet for students at the gateway to the campus.

Below: Computer Science Building; Researchers are drawn together in the multi level interactive foyer space.

The Saltire Centre, Glasgow Caledonian University. A learning interchange for students at the heart of the city centre campus.

Opposite: Bridges through the atrium interconnect the different learning areas with views to the cityscape.

A lot of university work typically consists of infill - slotting into the gaps, or renewing existing facilities. One such is the library/learning hub of the Saltire Centre at Glasgow Caledonian University, 2006 by Glasgow studio's John McManus, Colin Allan and Scott Mackenzie, which gives a new heart to this newish institution. In contrast, the 2008 Physics of Medicine building at the University of Cambridge by Chris Harding inserts a new multi-discipline teaching centre into one of the most ancient. 'Innovation through collaboration' is the motto of this new gateway to the famous Cavendish Laboratories.

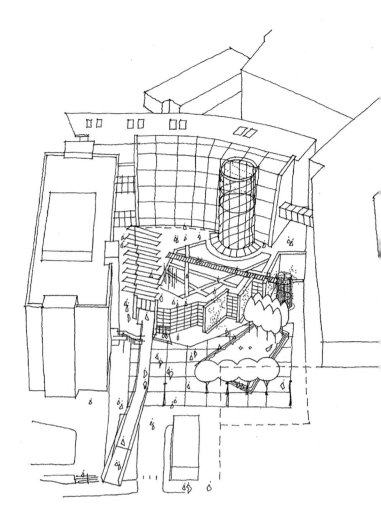

Right and below: The University of Cambridge, Faculty of Education, Homerton College. The city's most sustainable building. The 'timber house' research library, shaped around the garden, trees and sunpath.

Design preoccupations always tend to jump typologies. To what extent did the Scandinavian-humanist era ushered in by the University of Sunderland come to define the BDP look over the succeeding years? Of course, the practice will always deny having a house style and, by and large, it doesn't. But the organic approach - gentle shape - making if you will, allied to a variety of surface materials, colours and textures - has certainly come to be one of the more frequent aesthetic responses. You see it at the Cardiff Library where architects Adam Blacker, John Wakes and Richard Cowley together with John Bear deploy a rounded form to reduce bulk and mark the junction of two streets. A mix of glass curtain walling and brass-finished solid panels is used, depending on orientation. Sometimes a facade will curve over to form a roof, something you see at the Armada housing at Den Bosch in the Netherlands. This is a memorable centrepiece group of buildings to the new quarter of Paleiskwartier, in the historic Dutch city. Designed by Tony McGuirk, Benedict Zucchi and Chris Harding in London it has environmentally shaped, stainless steel roof forms that sit along a solar collector water course. The design for BDP's own Manchester studio, led by Gary Wilde and Stephen Redfern, does something similar for a different purpose. The environmental strategy influenced greatly by David Brennan and Chris Croly in Dublin, creates a solid stainless steel roof wrap over the south-facing street façade incorporating ventilation panels and controlled sunlight slots. The quieter world of the north-facing canal side is given a fully glazed elevation for calm light and views.

Cardiff City Library. A sustainable city landmark, set as an accessible island at the head of the main pedestrian street.

Left: A department store for learning and information. Daylit multi-layered learning territories at the heart of the city.

Above: The library as a children's learning house.

Below and right: Social interaction through juxtaposed balconies in the roof form and thresholds to wintergarden galleries at the entrance to each home.

Opposite: Long Houses and Tall Houses sit along the recreational/solar collector water space.

Bottom: Environmentally shaped roof forms offset turbulence from strong winds and enhance light from the big Dutch skies.

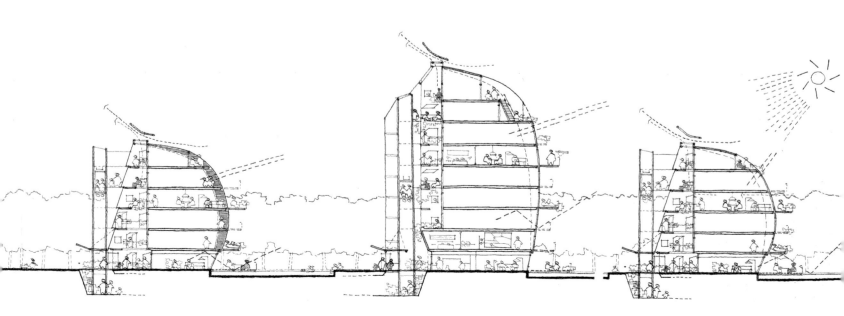

128

BDP's Manchester Studio.
The building form and
detail mediate the climate
conditions; warm and cool,
sunlight and daylight.

*BDP's Manchester Studio.
A building as regenerator,
bringing creative life to the
Piccadilly Basin district.*

This is not shape-making in the formal, icon-building sense, rather a way to break down the bulk of often quite large buildings. You see this approach in a series of hospital projects, including the Royal Alexandra Children's Hospital of 2008 in Brighton by Benedict Zucchi and Ray Cano Perez (winner of the Prime Minister's 'Better Public Building Award'), plus others in Birmingham and Yorkshire. It's in the nature of today's hospitals to be big, but they don't have to be inhuman. Given that BDP first started its existence in 1961 with the commission for the large Boston Pilgrim Hospital, it's had plenty of time to refine its thinking.

Royal Alexandra Children's Hospital, Brighton. A children's ark with multi-layered daylit activities, and views over the seaside.

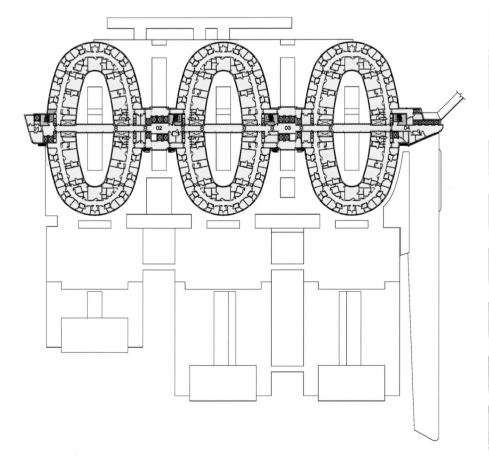

Queen Elizabeth Hospital, Birmingham. Ovate patient wards and bedrooms create identifiable, daylit, sunlit groupings.

Manchester's 2007 Abito apartments, an exercise in tunnel-form construction with a high degree of prefabrication, could easily have turned out as just another large slab block. But given apsidal ends, it became friendlier, less intrusive. Architects Gavin Elliott, Ian Palmer and interior designer Jasper Sanders further spawned a later sister Abito block in nearby Salford Quays. However, a more industrial, rectilinear (and simpler to plan) approach was adopted, and there the bulk was reduced by stepping the building down. Compared to the low-slung brick-and-tile blocks to either side of it, it has a suitably industrial scale and (with 290 apartments) density.

Right: Abito Housing, Manchester and Salford. Galleries with natural airflows form the access to the homes from the courtyard lightwell.

Below: Friends creating a first home in the city.

Below: Micro flat
inventiveness with central
service pods housing storage,
bathroom and kitchen. The
unencumbered layout creates
views, daylight and space all
around the small home.

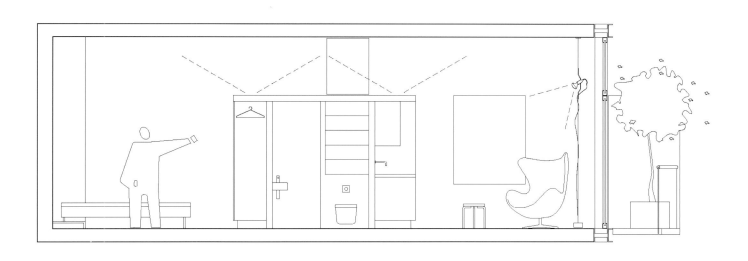

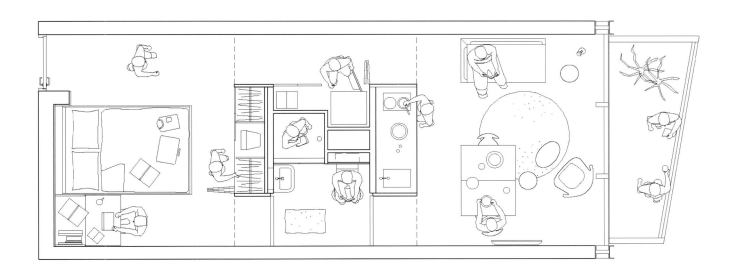

No, of course all of this relatively restrained shaping and paring of building form did not spring from one university commission, let alone one primary school. A mood of soft organicism swept across the practice, in tune with the times perhaps but also done in a recognisably BDP way. This cluster of projects does serve to demonstrate, beyond the obvious responses to the buildings' use, a desire to engage more gently with the urban realm as the 20th century turned to the 21st.

Left: Plans and sections indicate the micro flat grouping around the light and airwell with fabric roof canopy.

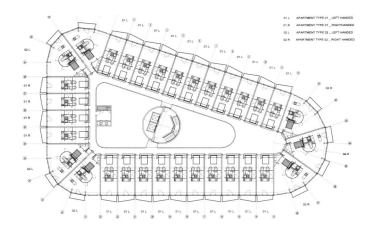

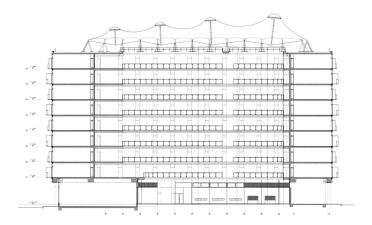

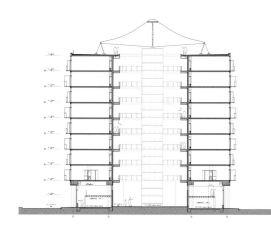

Catalyst projects 3: the Bigger Picture

At various times during BDP's history, the practice has made forays overseas. In the early days these were somewhat ad-hoc, and though some were on the back of a commission in a given country (such as Portugal) others were speculative. In this vein an early attempt to establish a base in the USA was abandoned and now seems naïve - at the time the US market was far less open to outsiders than it is today. A similar exercise in Saudi Arabia made more sense for a while, but the timing was wrong. This was the not unfamiliar story of a successful, expanding design organisation attempting to manage its growth by diversifying its markets, so becoming less dependent on the ups and downs of the volatile UK construction market.

The need for that was amply demonstrated in the crash of 1990-92 and the shake-up that followed. BDP had shrunk to less than half its late 1980s headcount (many rival firms fared worse or even disappeared entirely) while the first generation of partners had retired. The new leaner, younger BDP came up with a more pragmatic and much cheaper overseas plan: to form alliances with other European firms. A separate and loose international structure developed by successive chief executives Roger Horn and Roy Adams, with then chairman Ken Draper, formed alliances in France, Germany and Spain. They also set up a wholly-owned Irish office in then-booming Dublin, led initially by David Johnston from Belfast and lately by Dubliner David Brennan. This worked better than the early piecemeal approach, though it was by no means wholly successful and was to find itself shrinking even as, paradoxically, more overseas opportunities started to present themselves. In the 2000s (especially since the next big crash of 2008-10), the chief executive and chairman have promoted a wider strategic plan for international working. This is now given context by a central team of Peter Drummond, chief executive, David Cash, international director, John Parker, group finance director with Heather Wells and Bryn Fussell promoting and facilitating the initiatives of directors into identified new markets. In the main, these are supported by new commissions, in the Netherlands, China, India, and the United Arab Emirates. In 2010 alone, three new offices have now opened in three continents, in Abu Dhabi, New Delhi, and Shanghai with Toronto looking a future possibility.

St. Joseph's Bon Secours Hospital, Cork. The patient living areas are set like promontories into the sun overlooking the natural river valley.

Return to Health

By and large, BDP has always preferred to expand (and contract, when necessary) organically. But from time to time it makes an acquisition, always to strengthen itself in a particular discipline, typology, or geographic area. In its early to mid existence it had been strong in hospital design, only to move later into other areas such as retail. So early in the 2000s it bought specialist health practice Whicheloe MacFarlane. This new studio in Bristol, led by Keith Pavey and supported in Southampton and later Winchester by Adrian Hitchcock, was intended to bolster BDP's relaunch into healthcare at a time of large public investment in the sector, and gave it a more balanced regional coverage in the UK, especially the south and south west. Its office in the Netherlands came from a similar acquisition of long-term collaborators Khandekar, while its front door in the UAE results from its merger with long-established Gulf practice Syna. But more informal associations also continue, as with Groupe 6 in France, based in Paris and Grenoble, which again is strong in healthcare.

All this might sound drily organisational, but the proof is in the product. Thus we see, in the health sector, initially formed by healthcare champion Martin Sutcliffe, a resurgence of fresh projects from the early 2000s. Notable examples include the ovate Royal Alexandra Children's Hospital of 2007 in Brighton. Conceived as a 'Children's Ark' floating above the surrounding streets that press in on all sides, this forms a complete environment designed around the child, the parents and those who care for them. This is the product of a wholly interdisciplinary design process lead by Benedict Zucchi with Ray Cano Perez, engineers Michelle McDowell,

Michael Whitehurst, Kevin Featherstone with interiors, graphics and lighting by John Bear, Katharine Blankley, Richard Dragun, Marc Jenkins and Laura Bayliss. Later came the mighty new Queen Elizabeth Hospital in Birmingham which featured as a backdrop to the launch of the 2010 General Election campaign as the government focused on its stewardship of the National Health Service. The first patients were treated in June 2010, a month following that election. With 1231 beds, it is enormous. The design team was formed between the established Sheffield studio under David Clarke and the young Birmingham studio under Dan Smyth. But it is not a bureaucratic top-down building; led by architect Andrew Smith with Chris Green, Jennifer Meiring and John Tinner, the result is based on thorough-going consultation with everyone from those most involved - patients and their visitors - to the doctors, nurses and the health trust's clinical review groups. The aim was to establish common ground on what would constitute an ideal hospital. So while large, it does not sprawl, taking the form of a compact campus of three main interlinked sections. By grouping disease types, the distance patients have to move around is minimised, as is the number of healthcare professionals they have to meet. Aesthetically its principal curving towers carry an echo of early modernist sanatorium architecture. Behind those towers the bulk steps down in wide shallow terraces. It is a hospital with a sense of civic duty and importance.

This ambitious project took from 2004 to 2012 to design and build, at a construction cost of £559m. Not all are like that, though the impending £430m 800-bed Bristol Southmead 'superhospital' by Andrew Smith and Chris Green, which opens in 2014, comes close. No less valid, however, is the little St. Joseph's Hospital for the Bon Secours sisters outside Cork in Ireland. This 60-bed hospital by Benedict Zucchi and Tony McGuirk, is at a human scale with a village cluster layout, arranged along a curving street in a wooded hillside setting. It was completed in 2001 having cost a mere £6m. That, then, describes the range. In between you will find hospital projects - built or in the pipeline - at Wakefield Pinderfields, Queen Alexandra Hospital Portsmouth, Queen's Hospital Romford, Victoria Hospital Kirkcaldy, Centre for Teaching, Trauma and Tertiary Care in Brighton and Mothers' and Childrens' Hospital, Kiev. These all play variations on a planning theme which, tracked back, is to do with breaking down a large building into more manageable segments in a variety of ways, the kind of thinking that originally inspired the (rather different) Victorian Nightingale wards. Context and response vary hugely, from open landscaped campuses to landlocked urban sites.

Kiev takes this thinking to a new level. While many of the other large healthcare projects adopt a 'finger' plan of adjacent wings in various ways, Kiev's plan modifies this in a way more akin to an air terminal in that its five wings fan out from a central common area. However, in execution it could not be further from that typology, indeed being closer to the woodland village concept of St. Joseph's. Its full title is The All-Ukrainian Protection Centre for Mothers and Children, and true to its context and despite its considerable 250-bed size, it is inspired by Ukrainian dachas in the woods. Naturally ventilated, of sustainable materials and in tune with its surroundings, this is surely the direction we would all want healthcare to be heading. Dubbed locally 'The Enchanted Hospital', it is a product of BDP's long-term liaison with French architects Groupe 6. The team led by Neil Cadenhead in London formed a 3 pronged design attack with engineering designed by BDP in Belfast.

Such was the impact of BDP's return to the health sector, which would account for a large specialist practice in itself if you separated out all the professionals involved across the various studios. But if there is one thing that the practice has learned during its long history, it is not to become over-reliant on any one area. So while this very successful re-emergence into healthcare was going on (alongside the other sectors) another key skill was becoming apparent: masterplanning.

Urban Scale

Masterplanning is a word that can mean a variety of things, from the very specific to the remarkably vague. A masterplanner might also contribute all or some of the buildings in a district, or leave those entirely to others. A masterplanner might set up strict design criteria for those buildings, or just let a thousand flowers bloom. Plainly there is a difference between a competition-winning concept and a fully worked-out scheme. And to what extent does a masterplan differ from an old-fashioned comprehensive redevelopment strategy?

All this reached a pitch of public discussion in 2009 when the 42-acre Liverpool One retail district was shortlisted for the Stirling Prize. This marked a number of firsts: for instance retail is a sector that is usually a stranger to the architectural awards podium. This is not just the legacy of the old commercial architecture snobbery, but a response to the fact that each retailer has its own design ethos, normally carried out by specialist firms, which tends to reduce the impact of the overall architecture. Within your typical sealed shopping mall, with retailers visually jostling for your attention, architecture is well back in the mix. Liverpool One, however, is different. It is a district in itself. It puts right what had been a grievously run-down area which - despite the centrality implied by the L1 postcode - had previously felt like the rough edge of town. It re-establishes a ruptured street plan, helps reconnect the historic Albert Dock area to the centre, incorporates existing buildings and adds many others, contributed by a large and impressive roster of architects of all persuasions. It is open to the sky as city streets are, though there are also sheltered areas and arcades. It is in parts multi-level. It includes a five-acre public park and plenty of residential, offices and hotels as well as retail and leisure, including a large cinema complex, and the regional studios of the BBC. As is often the case, this project also formed an intense collaboration between people in BDP's different studios over different stages of development. The super size design team was led by architect Terry Davenport with Jaimie Ferguson, Stephen Gillham, Andy Teage, in Liverpool, landscape architects Phil Moss, Paul Taylor, Karen Howell, and lighting designer Laura Bayliss in Manchester, architect Jeremy Sweet, urbanist Richard Rees, and town planner Peter Drummond in London.

Left: Liverpool One.
The night time illumination accentuates the shop interiors, giving atmosphere to the new streets and visually connecting them to the historic part of the city.

Below and far left:
Perches to view the city and its people in sunny protected city spaces.

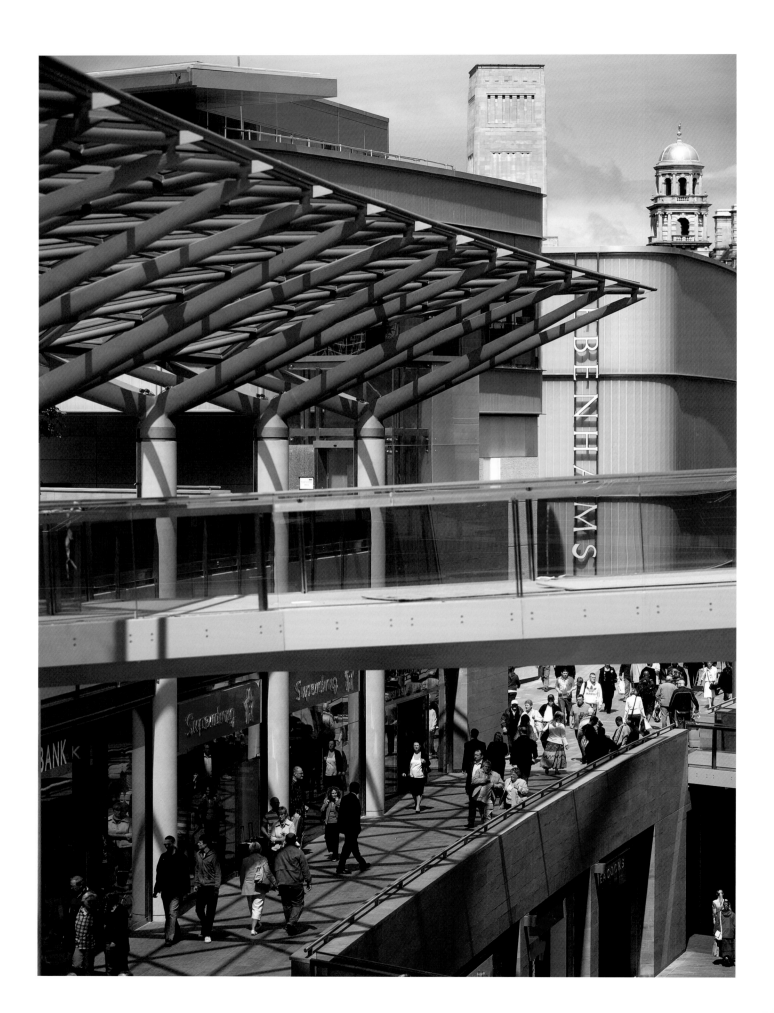

*Multi-layered open streets
stitch together the old
and new city routes at
different levels creating
three dimensional people
activity and movement.*

Such a project was unprecedented in the UK, and most other places as well. Effectively a large central part of a city - which in normal circumstances you might have expected to have been handled by the municipal authorities - was given to a private sector company, in this case Grosvenor Estates, to rescue. Essentially this was a recognition of the fact that this once great metropolis and seaport, Britain's fourth-largest city, had fallen into such a bad way that urgent remedial action was needed. Liverpool was rudderless and taking on water. Its population had halved since its peak in the 1930s, a decline that accelerated in the post-war years, was marked by the Toxteth riots of 1981, and despite various urban regeneration measures and short-term revivals was continuing at the turn of the 21st century. The old centre was largely shunned, though the former industrial quarter of the adjacent Ropewalks was reviving piecemeal successfully as a cultural district while the restored Albert Dock with its attractions was a tourist destination. Liverpool is an important university city, but the buildings are placed inland and uphill, closer to the two great cathedrals. Down in the commercial centre matters were once again becoming desperate.

By 2004 when this £1 billion project began, what started as the Paradise Project (named after Paradise Street) and was later named Liverpool One, was the last-chance saloon for this part of the city, a strategy to reverse the decline and bring people back not only into the centre from the suburbs, but from the great rival north west city of Manchester, only 30 miles away.

I have been lucky enough to see Liverpool at intervals from the industrial-dereliction days of the late 1970s, through the political turmoil and regeneration measures of the 1980s and 1990s, to the 'City of Culture' period leading to today. Visiting the city during and

after the opening of Liverpool One, the transformation was remarkable. Those who think that all retail centres are the same (it's true that too many are) will find food for thought here. At its most basic, it is a reversal of the old problem of a city centre shopping mall being a sealed box which does nothing for its surroundings: the Grosvenor team leader and urban champion, Rod Holmes, ensured that Liverpool One was not a sealed box and the project is everything to do with the grain of the city and its connections.

Of course it is not perfect - some parts work urbanistically better than others. Depending on your tastes, you will like some architects more than others. Of course it is dominated by retail - is now one of the top five retail centres in the UK. If you don't like shops and cafes and bars, go elsewhere. And there will always be a question mark over private ownership of previously public streets, even when full access is allowed. But Liverpool One, with its carefully contrived variety, succeeded. People flocked back into the centre, an average of 550,000 a week. It is not all one tempo - there are very busy parts, balanced by quiet corners that you might not realise are part of the same development. The overall consequence is that the standard has been raised significantly for other cities.

This notion of a new benchmark must have been in the judges' minds when Liverpool One landed on the Stirling shortlist. It was in fact not quite the first masterplan with multiple architects to get there (the Accordia housing development in Cambridge, which won the previous year, must take that honour) but this was on an unprecedented scale, with a roll-call of names as long as your arm but with BDP - which contributed its own buildings alongside all the others in its masterplan - leading the pack. It didn't win, but it became the most talked-about of the contenders.

The zig-zag stair winds its
way up the differing levels
in theatrical light form.

Liverpool One.
Chavasse Park.
Reintroducing the green
city park space linking
the commercial centre
of the city with its
historic waterfront.

Similar thinking is manifested elsewhere, as at the near-simultaneous Victoria Square in Belfast, Northern Ireland - a city with a historic connection to Liverpool. Still enormous at around half the size of Liverpool One, Victoria Square plays the same game of repairing the city fabric and opening it up to the waterfront, in this case the river Lagan. The difference is that previously its site was off-pitch rather than central, so that it extends rather than replaces an existing centre. Where Liverpool One has its heart in the form of its park, Victoria Square gathers its routes together beneath a Reichstag-inspired glass dome, 38 metres across, complete with observation decks from which to view the city. In this sense it is more overtly symbolic of regeneration, especially the economic upturn that followed the ending of the years of civil unrest in the city. The project interrelated concept design by Peter Coleman and Jeremy Sweet in BDP's London studio with the interdisciplinary design team in Belfast, led by studio chairman Norman Bennie with Doug Pilkington, Stephen Gallagher and engineers Paul Niblock, John Hutchinson, Andrew Cornett, Richard Smyth and John Lynch, director of cost and project planning. Incidentally BDP was no fair-weather arrival in the province, having had offices in Northern Ireland right through the dark days.

The start of the involvement here was the winning of the major planning commission for the Belfast urban and central area plans in 1966 led by architect and planner David Woods. A number of prominent figures in BDP helped to develop the office over the 40 year timeframe, including architect Bob Greenslade who led the design of the Northern Bank and Ulster University, town planner Roy Adams, later to become chief executive and David Johnston, environmental engineer, who expanded the office to a size which could take on Victoria Square.

Victoria Square, Belfast. Interlinking existing streets with new multi-level shopping streets, like the grand arcades of Europe.

The central dome creates a new public belvedere overlooking the city and its waterside setting.

Below and middle right: Cathedral Gardens, Manchester. A new green heart for the city's Millennium Quarter with themed lawns, trees, hard landscaped areas and water features, contrasting strongly with the more urban civic space around it.

Right: Cornmill Gardens, Lewisham. Links surrounding areas of the town centre and creates a safe and sustainable public place for both day and night time activity.

Left: Ladywell Fields, Lewisham. The significant transformation of this urban parkland has increased use and enjoyment, reduced crime and improved habitats for wildlife.

Bottom: Concert Square, Ropewalks, Liverpool. An area that has benefitted from a programme to radically improve the external environment of this historic but once neglected area.

This Belfast project, together with Liverpool One, ran contiguously with other projects of different types looking at improving the urban landscape in the centre of cities and also regenerating urban areas in the outer ring of cities like Manchester, London and Liverpool. BDP had again come to prominence in this work as one of the participants in the masterplan for central Manchester post the IRA bomb in 1996. This resulted in a major new urban space being created at Cathedral Gardens revitalising this end of the city between Victoria Station and the cathedral and forming the setting for the Urbis Building. The landscape architects and urbanist team of Paul Taylor, Karen Howell, Francis Glare, Dan Smyth and Peter Shuttleworth spanned the masterplanning work. In Liverpool they also took forward the urban regeneration masterplan of the Ropewalks district, uphill from Paradise Street, which was to become the new Liverpool One. In London a similar profession make up team with urban lighting to the fore brought regenerative new places in Walthamstow and Lewisham in particular, led by Andrew Tindsley with Mehron Kirk, Martin Savage, Tessa O'Neill, Laura Bayliss and Martin Lupton. At the other end of the socio-economic pole BDP is undertaking the public realm work in Mayfair, with the design led by Nick Edwards following a report by urban design guru, Jan Gehl from Copenhagen.

Movement patterns

Working at city scale was of course not a new thing. Right back at the start of BDP's existence had come the new 1960s university campuses, a typology which returned in the next big university expansion period of the 1990s and 2000s. Some industrial projects, from ICI to Opel, had also been at campus scale. One of the biggest of them all, however, came about twice: first in the 1970s, then in the 1980s, finally being completed in the mid 1990s. This was the UK's Channel Tunnel Terminal at Folkestone.

As first conceived in the early 1970s, the Channel Tunnel was going to be a state-funded project. In 1975 BDP designed the preliminary layout for the English terminal at Cheriton near Folkestone, for the Ministry of Transport. But the government found it had only enough money to fund the supersonic airliner Concorde, or the Tunnel, but not both. They chose Concorde, so the project was put on ice in 1975 and had to wait a decade, by which time it was a wholly private-sector affair.

Of the various groups bidding to build it, one - the eventual winner - adhered closely to the original 1975 strategy and called in BDP to refresh its existing terminal masterplan, thus having a head start over its rivals. Since this scheme involved dedicated car-carrying shuttle trains as well as through expresses and freight trains, the design of the terminal was generated by the need for continuous movement of the shuttles around a large covered loop track, combined with a seamless integration of the road network. Five kilometres long by 750 metres wide, with a total area of 140 hectares, the terminal is nonetheless only one quarter the size

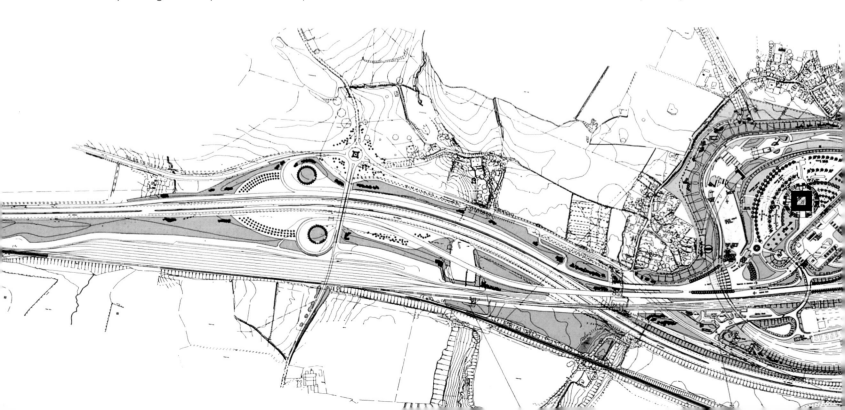

Channel Tunnel UK Terminal, Folkestone.
An ordered layout for a unique road
and rail international transport system
is integrated into the natural setting of
England's South Downs.

of its identical capacity French equivalent. Squeezed between a chalk escarpment and a motorway, in an Area of Outstanding Natural Beauty, it could not waste space or be over-intrusive. All the many disciplines in BDP were involved on the project, which includes a low-key family of 19 buildings plus other structures. The design concept led by architect Bob Smart and engineer Jim Armstrong, with Tony McGuirk, Chris Sayers, director of landscape architecture Janet Jack, engineering Alan Watson, Arnold Aarons and cost management Alan Swash, brought coherence to the design for what was to be the UK's largest design and build project of its time. It must be said that engineering considerations came first, since its function is to be a giant marshalling yard with a public interface. From an architectural point of view, this was a very large design-build project, so the buildings had to

be designed with that (then rough) process in mind. The public buildings are white like the local chalk, ranging from the tollbooth canopies for arriving motorists to the main amenity building, designed as a structure that visually floats in the landscape, offering views out from its corners, marked by an asymmetrical tensile-fabric roof angled towards France.

Everything about the UK Terminal is enormous but it eschews monumentality in favour of understatement, on the grounds that the true monument is the surrounding hilly landscape. Under intense public scrutiny from first to last, it required skills beyond design: BDP had to present to government committees and local residents alike. Smoothly in operation now for well over 15 years, its greatest achievement perhaps is its self-effacing nature: it just gets on with the job, proving itself over and over.

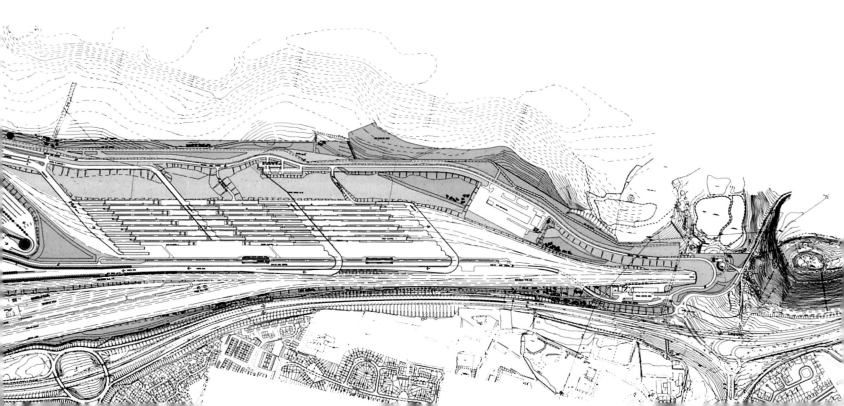

The Channel Tunnel Terminal led onto other transport infrastructure projects with an equally long gestation period. Next up, in 1992, was Crossrail, London's east-west express train system involving several complex new underground stations across the centre of the city. For the first designs, BDP put together a collaboration of Tony McGuirk with Ralph Erskine. Together they developed a common organic language for the stations, both for the excavated container of the main construction (more usually a rectangular box) and also at platform level which departed from the normal engineering solution of a large-diameter bored tube to offer something more ovoid. The fluid dynamics of people movement were echoed by the below-ground architecture.

Sadly this was not to be. Crossrail was put on hold for many years, and when it finally began to be built in 2010, the various stations with their above ground developments had changed, and construction was more conventional. However BDP retained an involvement in this key infrastructure improvement, with the design of the Whitechapel interchange in East London by Robert Keefe and Chris Langston. With an intersecting overbridge design incorporating a green roof, this will connect Crossrail with the existing underground and overground services, and is due to open in 2014. Projects such as this - another would be the 2007 station in the Dublin expansion settlement of Adamstown - have great economic and social impact on their communities.

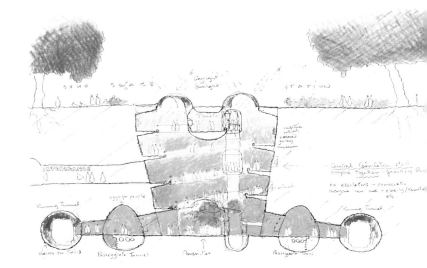

Crossrail Central London Stations. Atria set in the ground take passengers within daylit subterranean spaces from the city squares to the platforms 30 metres below.

Piccadilly Station, Manchester, reshaped as an intercity transport terminus where daylight and multi-level activity enhance the passenger experience.

More conventional perhaps - though it involved the rethinking of a surprisingly large fragment of city - was the much-garlanded Piccadilly Station in Manchester with its new twin-level concourse, completed in 2002. This is the main terminus of England's second city. The spur to its regeneration was the Commonwealth Games held in Manchester, as a result of which it was among the first of Network Rail's main terminals to be brought properly up to date for the new century. The design led by architect Peter Shuttleworth, with Peter Jenkins and Richard Elsdon, achieved many things from painstaking restoration of the original 19th century fabric, through to the deployment of lightweight ETFE translucent foil 'pillows' for the roof of the large new concourse building. The station's former 1960s taxi approach ramp was given over to pedestrians, new servicing was provided from the building's undercroft and offices for railway staff and a new taxi node were established at ground level on the southern flank of the building, plus a better connection to the Manchester tram network.

This was a pioneering project, establishing a template for much-needed railway station expansion as intercity passenger numbers steadily grew: in the UK they are now back up to peak 1920s levels, and a large-scale programme of intercity station upgrades is under way. The Piccadilly project proved that all this could be done on a constrained urban site - even working the new concourse building around the base of an existing tower block.

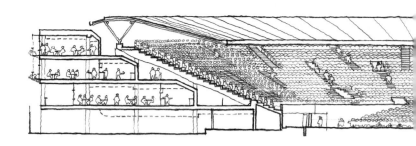

The serious matter of sport

As masterplans go, few were more thorough than BDP's remaking of the All England Lawn Tennis and Croquet Club - better known as Wimbledon. The sheer numbers of people moving around and between the courts during the Grand Slam fortnight each year is staggering. Yet at the outset of this phased project in 1992, Wimbledon had changed comparatively little since the 1950s. It had slipped so badly behind its international rivals that it even considered moving the venue out of London altogether. It had the typical problem of long-established sporting venues: increasing demand for new facilities and larger courts, coupled with a congested, landlocked site. What to do?

The masterplanning response was to go back to first principles and consider the complex as if it were a country house (Centre Court) in a landscaped setting with subsidiary buildings. Then, in a phased programme running more than a decade, the overall circulation was sorted out including underground vehicle servicing throughout, separation of public entrances from staff and competitors, a new 11,000-seat No 1 Court to the north (it had previously been tacked on the side of Centre Court) and several other buildings including the all-important Millennium Building housing the tennis players themselves, the media, all the officials for the tournament from ball boys and girls to umpires, and the members of the club with all their guests and VIPs. Extensive landscaping includes the creation of the famous, Henman Hill, now known as Murray's Mound, with its giant outdoor screen. Some of the new building is scarcely visible, being essentially a raised ground plain

Below: The Wimbledon Tennis Championships. The masterplan overview showing the concept of Tennis in an English Garden.

Righ: The circular form of the New No 1 court sets new standards for viewing and playing international tennis.

that exploits the slope of this valley site: while even the prominent dish of the No 1 Court is kept low-profile by being sunk into the ground so as not to upstage Centre Court. The design accentuates new terraces and vantage points as an essential part of the overall experience of enjoying the tennis scene, its competitors and spectators.

This project once again was a result of BDP's extensive interdisciplinary team's ability to span a complicated, long term development, whose whole had to be greater than the sum of the parts - that is to create a place and an experience. A host of profession leaders came together here. Masterplanners and urbanists Richard Saxon, Richard Rees, Peter Drummond, Sandra Roebuck and Tessa O'Neill, architects Tony McGuirk, Roger Stollery and Chris Harding, engineers Derek Pike,

Michelle McDowell, Bob Spittle and Andrew Swain-Smith, landscape architects Andrew Tindsley and Martin Jones and interior designers Rodney Cooper and Martin Cook, spanned the project phases over the ten year timeframe. What was also telling about this project was the way it was won against high-grade competition. This was not just the design of a sports building, or even several: it required a greater level of experience in everything from crowd movement through retail and leisure design to landscape and project management. The analogy drawn may have been with a country house estate - Tennis in an English Garden, but actually the firm's previous experience in university campuses, shopping centres, cultural venues and the urban realm counted for as much as the rural/ urban idyll or even its previous sports portfolio.

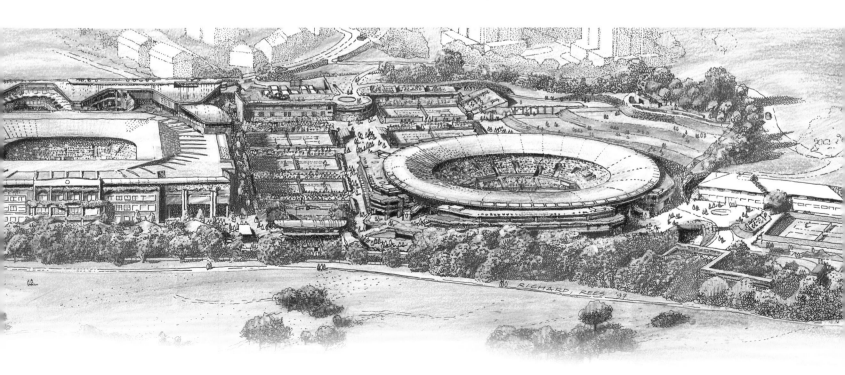

Below: The Wimbledon Tennis Championships, Masterplan. The reordered sequence of pedestrian movement between the events creates one third more space for the spectators to enjoy the tennis.

Below: The Millennium Building houses the tennis players, the international press, the tournament officials and the tennis club members on an array of 'lido' terraces and lawns overviewing the tennis courts.

Right: The Grand National Development, Aintree. A continuous experience of watching horses and watching people.

Below: Theatre grandstands and central Saddlebar create the spectator backdrop to the greatest steeplechase in the world.

After this, it was no surprise to find a number of other follow-up tennis venues came BDP's way, sometimes in collaboration with others: Australia's Olympic Tennis Centre of 2000, the Athens Olympic Tennis Centre of 2004, and the competition-winning, and recently completed Guangzhou International Tennis Centre of 2007 led by Richard Rees. Meanwhile the skills gleaned at all these venues and the interdisciplinary approach crossed over into other sports: the masterplan, new grandstands and parade ring of 2008 at Aintree Racecourse for the Grand National was the next big one with the design bringing together Tony McGuirk in London and Gavin Elliott, Andrew Capewell, Richard Elsdon and Phil Simcock in Manchester. Gavin Elliott and Andrew Capewell went on to masterplan Lancashire County Cricket's Old Trafford Ground, including the design of the hospitality and events building known as The Point, completed in 2010. With a vast column-free internal space, this oxide-red box overlooks the famous ground and hovers over spectator seating for 25,000 people. Its daytime character is transformed into a theatrical night time venue with lighting effects by designer Brendan Keely.

What is true of all these venues is that the design work extends for a considerable distance beyond the boundaries of individual buildings. The concentrated nature of sport is balanced by the diffuse needs and movement patterns of large audiences, something that has held true ever since the Romans built the Colosseum in Rome.

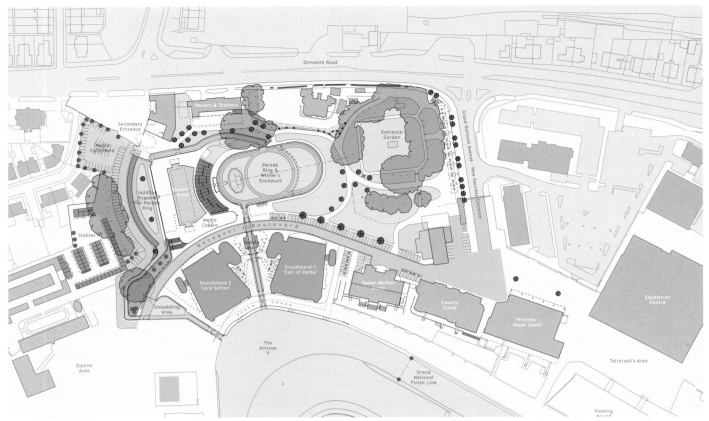

Above: The Grand National Development Masterplan. Integrates parade ring activities, grandstands and hospitality lawns to create a special setting for steeplechasing.

Grandstands designed as theatres linked by bars and cafes, which overlook the horses entering the course.

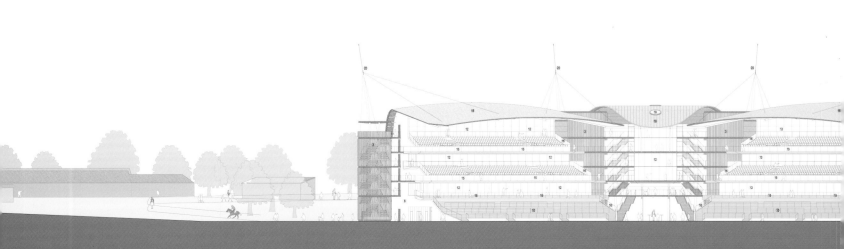

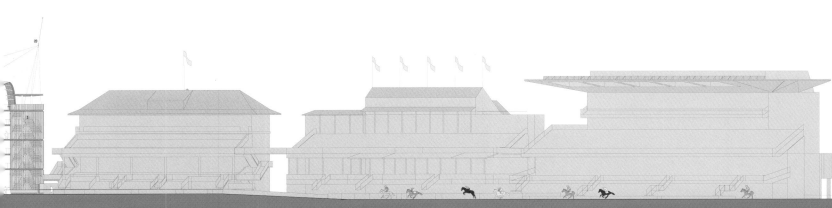

The Point Old Trafford, Lancashire County Cricket Club. A conference and events venue, gives shelter to the grandstand and a gigantic window onto the cricket.

Right: A night time venue with theatrical lighting effects.

Bottom: Section through the overall masterplan. Events, hospitality and hotel are integrated with spectator viewing.

Conclusions: Out in the world

A glance at the work being handled by BDP at the time of writing reveals an interesting pattern: the practice's experience of large-scale urban design is now increasingly in demand around the world. Consider, for instance, the work in China: the Nanjing Medical University in Jiangsu, with its design team led from Glasgow by John McManus, the Sanshui district of Foshan near Guangzhou led by Stephen Gillham with architect Tao Wang from the Manchester studio, and Ikea-anchored shopping developments in Beijing, Wuxi near Shanghai, and Wuhan, further east, conceived by Jeremy Sweet, with architects Sebastien Pollet and Jeremy Farrington and engineers John Roycroft, James Hepburn and lighting designer Mark Ridler. The scale of these Chinese developments is telling, but comes with a strong environmental component. The Foshan cultural and civic quarter, for instance, is designed to integrate with a rich landscape, planned around three watercourses: one central and formal, one a meandering leisure resource in a new park, the third in a quieter area devoted to wildlife. All lead down to the two main large civic buildings on the main riverfront.

The Nanjing Medical University, which won an international design competition, is relatively more modest: a pair of large new university buildings, again on the waterfront, with no hinterland as part of the scheme. But once again, it is designed to maximise the surrounding lakeland environment, balancing this with its own internal gardens, a necessity in what can be a harsh climate.

Masterplan proposals for Foshan, Guangdong Province, China. The natural environment has been the driver for the regeneration masterplan of this extensive civic quarter of the Sanshui District of Foshan city.

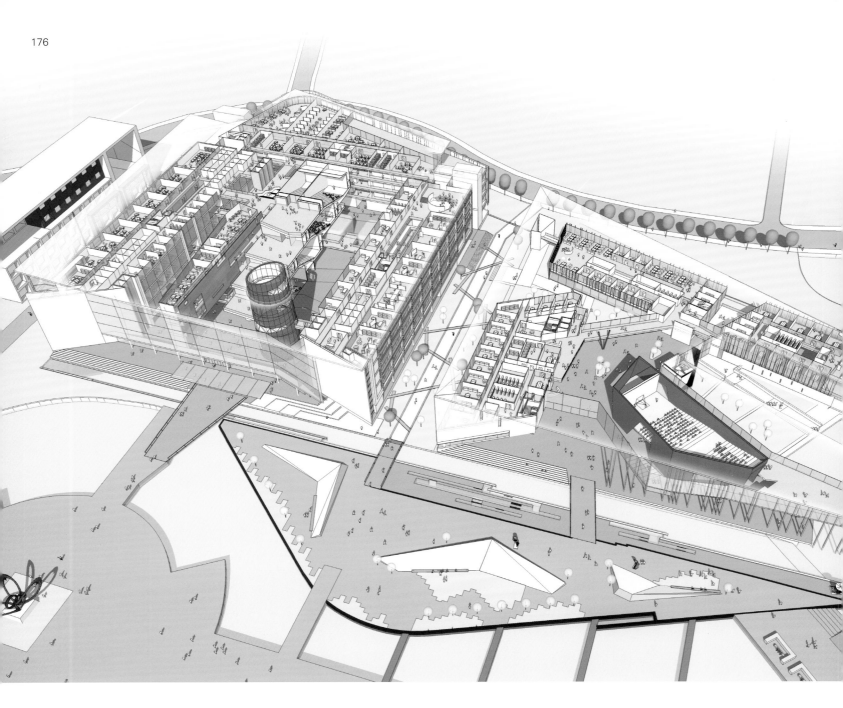

Above and right: Nanjing Medical University, Jiangsu, Province, China. A strong architectural form that unites the two new buildings, a teaching and research building and an administrative building, and responds to the landscape setting providing a dramatic symbol for the university's new campus.

Three major buildings, Foshan's central archive, library and urban exhibition hall, all housed under a single roof inspired by the petal form of a Chinese lily.

As for the large IICG (Inter Ikea Centre Group) developments, which are all anchored by an Ikea store, forget any notion you may have had of the European version of this Swedish retailer. The largest of the schemes, for Beijing, is on the appropriate scale for that city where everything, from ancient temples to its opera house and airport, is huge: something approaching a Buckminster Fuller dream of a complete enclosed, daylit city environment, covering 200,000 square metres on three levels. The smallest, at Wuhan, is half this size, which is still very considerable. Never forget that retail has been a strong strand of BDP's work ever since the 1970s. One aspect in particular of retail design - the dynamics of people-movement, the even spread of footfall throughout a retail area in order to maximise passing trade for every shop, café or cinema, the means of arrival and departure - has had substantial spin-off effect in other mass-audience projects ranging from sport to transport, cultural centres to schools. People are people, and when many of us are gathered and moving together, then you need designers who understand us, our habits and foibles.

Below: IICG, Beijing, China. A view of the Beijing development highlighting the covered street retail circuit. The building connects directly with the new light railway station as do all the IICG developments in China.

India, where BDP has its office in New Delhi, offers a similar level of activity: particularly when it comes to the business of a manufacturing-led economy turning increasingly to the knowledge economy. Hence the Nirlon Knowledge Park in Mumbai, where a nine-hectare former textile complex is in the process of being transformed by Shyam Khandekar into a landscaped technology park, complete with café in a leftover cooling tower. The commission here was masterplanning and landscape led, with the first phase completed in 2008. A bioscience campus in Hyderabad set in a rocky valley is also planned, but next up will be Bombay Boulevard, a complete city block incorporating a shopping mall and apartments, but opening up into an urban park. The design led by Adrian Price and John Wakes in London with Manisha Bhartia and Akshay Khera in New Delhi, creates a terraced mall, inhabited inside and out and heavily planted, which steps down to the park with its stream and leisure building. The term urban oasis is frequently misused, but it describes what's going on here well.

Top right: Nirlon Knowledge Park, Mumbai. A waterpark landscape setting for business and research transforming a former textile complex.

Bottom right: Bombay Boulevard, Mumbai. A new mixed use urban block with water courses and leisure activities, creating an urban oasis within this district of the city.

Overseas markets are opening up in places that would once have been considered very unlikely. The economic and cultural growth of Libya, for instance (disrupted at the time of writing by social unrest), is demonstrated by BDP's design of ten new universities across the country, which are all now under construction. All different and varying in size, they each represent a new settlement, from teaching faculties through to student and staff residences. This challenging series of projects brings together the full interdisciplinary design team with David Cash, Ged Couser and Ian Purser, Dan Smyth, and Stephen Marshall in masterplanning and architecture, engineers Keith Crossley and Michael Whitehurst with sustainability by David Ritter.

At times, when describing such projects, you have to pinch yourself. In the UK in the 1960s, doing two universities simultaneously, as BDP did at Bradford and Surrey, was a big deal. But ten, all at once, and on a rapid programme? It would have been tempting to design a standard repeatable model, but that was not the response in the 1960s beyond certain components, nor is it now. Conditions, topography, climate, all vary and so do the designs, seen as variations on a theme.

On the scale of the big urban plan, typologies merge. Everything becomes mixed-use, if often with a greater emphasis on some uses than others. But with the multiple educational model, as now evolving in the Middle East, it's the different business of large scale, single function. While in Libya it is universities, in Abu Dhabi it may well be schools that may form the catalyst for the practice to show its interdisciplinary colours, evolving the strategies for the British school building boom of the 2000s. In other parts of the Middle East and North Africa the big urban plan with mixed typologies like Salmiya in Kuwait led by urbanist Francis Glare, looks likely to be the main driving force that moves from urban design to building design.

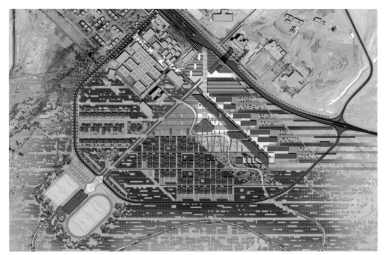

University Masterplans Libya. The designers use generic thinking interlinked with a climatic and contextual response to the different settings of each university campus.

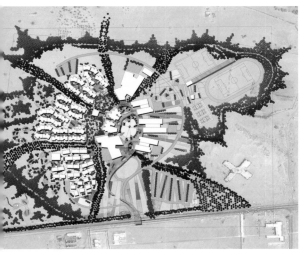

It is one of the truisms of architecture that if you can design a good house, you can design a good anything. A house is surprisingly complex and multifunctional, a city in miniature. A city is a house at urban scale. All built environment designers, then, if they are worth their salt, must long to tackle, if not a complete new city, then at least a complete new city district. Many of the projects in this book attain or approach that scale. In the Netherlands in particular - an entirely designed nation in its relationship of humans to land - this has often been the mindset: don't think individual buildings, think of the complete picture. The Palace Quarter (Paleiskwartier) in 's-Hertogenbosch, a remaking of a former industrial quarter on the wrong side of the city's railway tracks, is an example, originally masterplanned by Shyam Khandekar and Liesl Vivier. BDP Khandekar is now of course one practice, and the Dutch masterplanning work continues at Rhenen Vogelenzang, the 'pavilions in the park' modern-housing landscape of Lelystad's Noordzoom, and a similar project to Paleiskwartier, a few miles down the road in Tilburg led by Shyam Khandekar and Jeroen Bleijs.

Top: This old industrial sand reclamation pit has been transformed into a picturesque setting for a new settlement.

Right: Paleiskwartier, Den Bosch. The Netherlands. Completing the core of the city: the new quarter next to the international station creates a total city environment of workplace, living place and learning place with shops and recreation, side by side with the historic city.

Opposite: Tilburg Central Masterplan. The Netherlands. High rise housing with parkland recreation creates a relaxed new living style in the station area of the city.

It is not often, however, that you are given the chance to reinvent the whole idea of the city with not one but several urban districts. This is the case at the international competition-winning Seaton New Town on the eastern edge of Toronto. This masterplan, led by BDP's head of sustainability Richard Buckingham, with Richard Rees, Tony McGuirk, Howlan Mullally and Keith Watson, creates a new settlement for 70,000 residents with 36,000 working in green industries. To give a scale comparison, the mighty city-centre Liverpool One development in Britain covers an area of 17 hectares, while the entire new city of Milton Keynes, first planned in the 1960s, occupies an area roughly three times the size of Seaton New Town at

8,900 hectares. With clients including both government agencies and Canadian developers, Seaton is to be a phased development over 20 years, with construction likely commencing in 2011-2012. Various districts may at first seem somewhat fanciful, including the evocative 'Dancer' and 'Angel' districts. But the what-if thinking is now being distilled down into designs that will work

The **Dancer** district

Above: A living high street for each district, with homes, shops, vertical schools and entertainment, within a short walking distance from the edge of the neighbourhood.

Left and opposite: Identifiable districts, related to topography and climate with north south orientation of major street pattern, integrate with the natural watershed ecology as commons and neighbourhood parks for the community and local schools.

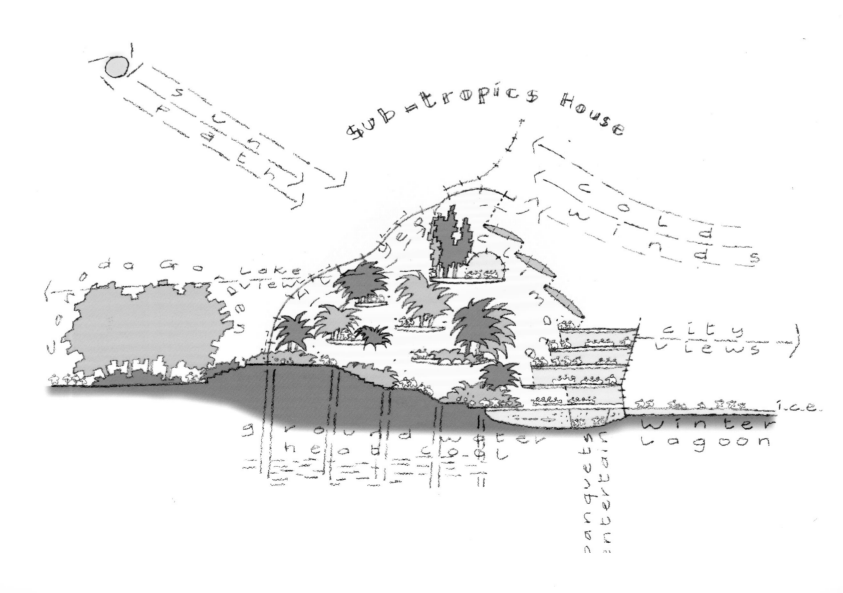

pragmatically and commercially as well as aesthetically and environmentally. The integration of nature and agriculture into a wholly sustainable plan for Seaton has also been taken further by the design team in their ideas to be published for Ontario Place, an island in Lake Ontario - with even vertical vineyards and vertical schools in biospheres. Here vertical kitchen gardens, orchards, and proposals for botanical gardens with anaerobic digesters demonstrate the idea of a climatic all year round community. This is the exact opposite of sprawling, land-gobbling Milton Keynes, promoting an ecologically - designed town where a good density of development allows maximum retention of natural landscape, with that landscape penetrating right into and through the built-up areas. A fully-integrated public transport system is planned that allows automated car-guidance systems as well as more conventional (but low carbon) mass transit.

Left: Wintergarden
biosphere for all year
round activity, visually
and actively connected
to the seasonal changes
of Lake Ontario.

Above: Ontario
Place Competition,
Toronto. Compact
climatic city idea.

These ideas for Seaton New Town, form a good place to end this book on the 50th anniversary of BDP, for several reasons. Here you have the disciplines and areas of expertise in different building types coming together in a masterplan as never before. Here you have an important competition win in a country where the practice has previously built nothing. Here you have a European urbanistic sensibility called in to suggest new ways forward for the New World. Here you have a place full of ideas and opportunities, that will lead the practice in directions that may surprise it. Whatever Seaton New Town may mean for the practice alongside all its other work around the world, this is critical: it is, emphatically, not more of the same.

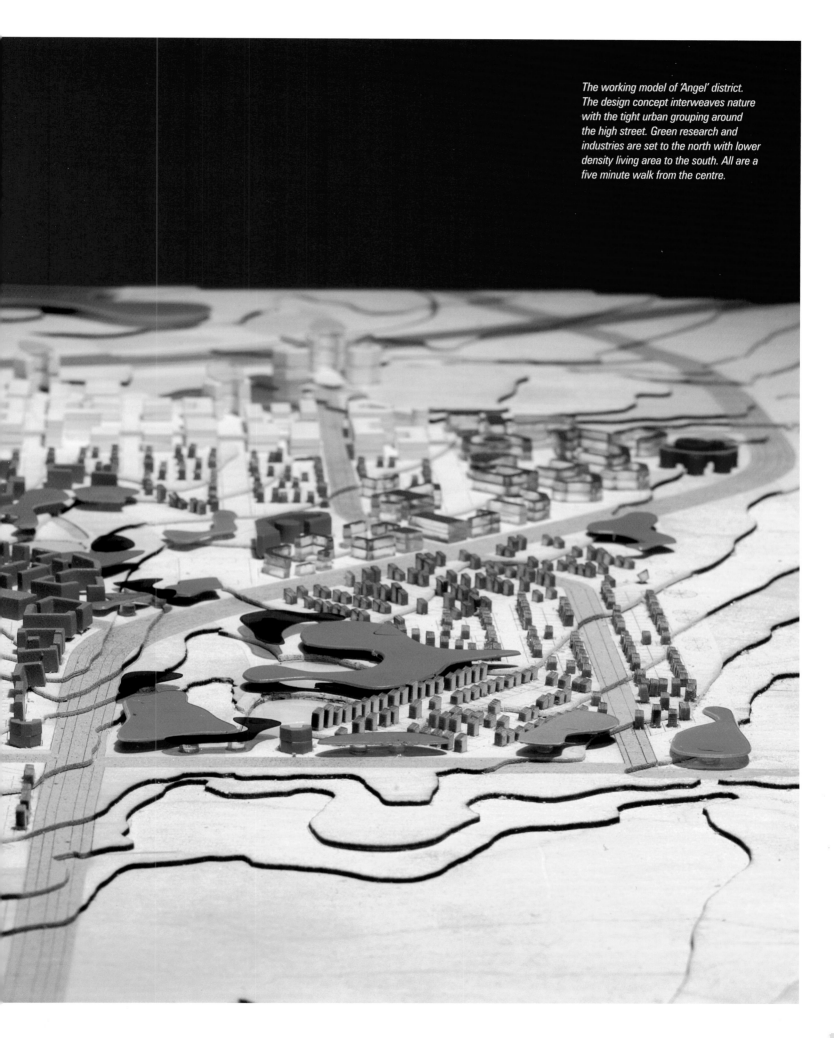

The working model of 'Angel' district.
The design concept interweaves nature
with the tight urban grouping around
the high street. Green research and
industries are set to the north with lower
density living area to the south. All are a
five minute walk from the centre.

Picture Credits

Photographers
Stephen Ambrose
Roger Ball
David Barbour
Richard Bryant
Martin Charles
Chris Christodoulou
Commission Air
Sanna Fisher-Payne
Keith Gibson
Dennis Gilbert
Roland Halbe
Martine Hamilton Knight
Keith Hunter
Phil Mastores
Anderson McMeekin Photography
Paul McMullin
David Millington
John Mills Photography
Andrew Moore
Luis Filipe Oliveira
Roger Park
Jermey Preston
QA photos
Jason Randall
Rupert Truman
Winter & Kidson, Preston
Charlotte Wood

Picture libraries
Fiona Adams © Getty Images
Central Press © Getty Images
© Richard Cooper, Photoflex for Urban Splash
© Courtauld Institute of Art
© imagebroker.net / SuperStock
Popperfoto © Getty Images
Graeme Robertson © Getty Images
Gary Stone © Getty Images

Other
© Boeing Images
Scootering Jon Stevens © Penguin Books
© VG Bild-Kunst Bonn/DACS London, supplied
by Bauhaus-Archiv Berlin/ photo Markus Hawlik